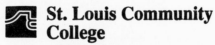

THE LAUREL
AND
HARDY
SCRAPBOOK

THE LAUREL AND HARDY SCRAPBOOK

Jack Scagnetti

JONATHAN DAVID PUBLISHERS
MIDDLE VILLAGE, N. Y. 11379

THE LAUREL AND HARDY SCRAPBOOK
by
Jack Scagnetti

Copyright © 1976
by
Jonathan David Publishers

Jonathan David Publishers, Inc.
68-22 Eliot Avenue
Middle Village, New York 11379

Library of Congress Cataloging in Publication Data

Scagnetti, Jack.
  The Laurel and Hardy scrapbook.

  1. Laurel, Stan. 2. Hardy, Oliver Norvell, 1892-
1957. I. Title.
PN2287.L285S25   791'.092'2 [B]   76-6566
ISBN 0-8246-0207-2

Printed in the United States of America

ACKNOWLEDGMENTS

The author is most grateful to the following for their assistance and cooperation:

Academy of Motion Picture Arts and Sciences and its Margaret Herrick Library; Norm Blackburn, Eddie Brandt's Saturday Matinee, Larry Byrd, Larry Edmunds Book Store, Richard Feiner, Dore Freeman, Hank Jones, *Los Angeles Times,* Lucille Hardy Price, Ben Price, Joe Rock, Murray Rock, Sons of the Desert clubs, Bob Villard and Harry Von Zell. Thanks are also extended to the following motion picture studios: Fortezza Films and Les Films Sirius, Larry Harmon Pictures Corporation, MGM, Hal Roach Studios, RKO Radio, Twentieth Century-Fox, and United Artists.

We gratefully acknowledge the cooperation of Larry Harmon, president of Larry Harmon Pictures Corporation, exclusive owners of the characters and likenesses of, and merchandising rights to, LAUREL AND HARDY, who has done so much to perpetuate their memory.

All of the photographs of Laurel and Hardy related to the Hal Roach motion pictures are reproduced by permission of Hal Roach Studios, Inc., copyright © Richard Feiner and Company, Inc.

Laurel and Hardy in Jitterbugs, *made in 1943.*

To
Lucille Hardy Price
and
Ben Price

Laurel and Hardy in Air Raid Wardens, *an MGM film.*

Contents

Introduction

Many middle-aged people have fond childhood memories of spending Saturday afternoons watching zany Stan Laurel and Oliver Hardy comedies at neighborhood theaters. Oh, what fun! How pandemonium would break loose the moment the familiar Laurel and Hardy theme song was played! Everyone in town knew when a Laurel and Hardy two-reel comedy was playing at their local movie house; the stars' names were boldly featured on the marquee. But many children merely referred to them as "fats" and "skinny," not caring who was Stan and who was Ollie.

It was the children of the late 1920s and early 1930s who *discovered* Stan Laurel and Oliver Hardy. They chose them as their favorite comedians and passed the word on to succeeding generations. Post-World War II children became familiar with the comedy team when Laurel and Hardy films were shown on television. They, too, loved them.

Laurel and Hardy were easily recognizable. They complemented each other perfectly—not only physically, but personality-wise as well. There stood thin-framed Laurel with his elongated face, blank expression, and wild, unruly hair. And next to him, firmly planted, was heavy-set Hardy with his tiny mustache and funny spit-curl bangs showing below his derby hat. Stan's flip-flop walk and Ollie's courtly southern gentleman manners made them distinctive characters. Laurel, always blamed for creating problems, would burst into tears during moments of extreme stress, while Hardy invariably aimed an exasperated appeal for help directly at the camera. The plot was always the same: Laurel and Hardy were two *nice* people, who would never accomplish anything because they were both so dumb. But they were unaware that they were dumb. It was this endearing naivete—this lack of awareness, more than their stupidity, that attracted fans and made them stars. The simplicity of their slapstick gags, and the dignity and good taste which they always maintained, disarmed audiences world-wide. The situations in which they became involved reminded viewers of their own lives. They laughed at Laurel and Hardy, but they were also laughing at themselves.

Today, Laurel and Hardy are recognized as masters of the comedic art. Ironically, in their prime, Laurel and Hardy were ignored by the critics. They were not considered to be in the same league as the great artists of the day who included Charlie Chaplin, Buster Keaton, Harold Lloyd and the Marx Brothers. And yet, today, three decades after the creation of their last regular series of comedy films, film critics agree that the twenties and thirties would not have been the same without the madcap antics of Laurel and Hardy. They all agree that Laurel and Hardy made a contribution to screen comedy that was both important and unique.

Several years ago, Hal Roach, producer of most of their films, was asked about the revived interest in Laurel and Hardy: "It's because there's a lack of their kind of comedy. People appreciate them more now because they haven't got any competition. Nobody's doing what they did. It seems to me that for the last four or five years people have been laughing at things that aren't funny just because they're dying to laugh."

One critic, in commenting on Laurel and Hardy's popularity with children, stated:

"The older folk often expressed the opinion that they were silly and childish. The youngsters knew better; they weren't childish, they were grown men reacting to the frustrating situations of life with the innocence, trust, occasional cruelty, but perennial optimism of children. Kids never want to grow up. They are reassured and happy when they find adults who have the ability to remain children."

There was much love in the films of Laurel and Hardy. And the "love generation" of the 1960s was responsible for the beginning of a revival of interest in the comedians. The public requested that the comedians' films be shown again. The cult which was forming soon grew and spread, and it continues to grow. A young soldier at Fort Leavenworth, Kansas went so far as to sell a pint of blood to earn the price of a ticket to a Laurel and Hardy double feature.

A Peace Corps volunteer in Africa hitchhiked some 250 miles to Nairobi to see a half-hour Laurel and Hardy short. In 1971, the *Wall Street Journal* reported that Tom Sefton, president of San Diego Trust & Savings Bank, dragged himself out of bed many mornings at 3:00 a.m. to watch 90 minutes of Laurel and Hardy on television's *Late, Late Show*.

Today, several television stations run the comedians' films regularly. Laurel and Hardy film festivals draw large audiences in many countries, even in Afghanistan, Ghana and India. A photograph of the two men was seen on mainland China where the Chinese revere them, and consider them symbolic of their country: Hardy representing the rotund and wise Mandarin; Laurel, the humble, undernourished peasant who bears life's burdens with courage.

The Sons of the Desert, a Laurel and Hardy buff club, now has more than 25 chapters. Laurel and Hardy mementos, including theater posters and lobby cards of the 1920s and 1930s, are sold at high prices. Several books have been written about Laurel and Hardy and more are in preparation.

Stan Laurel and Oliver Hardy achieved more universal appeal than most film stars. In the Middle and Far East and in India, their pictures are popular and can be shown without dubbing the dialogue. Everyone can relate to their slapstick routines. World statesmen including Winston Churchill and Josef Stalin found their antics relaxing, and held private screenings of the team's films during World War II. Marshall Tito continues to view their movies to this day.

Presented here, in this volume, are the individual biographies of Laurel and Hardy, and their story as a team. *The Laurel and Hardy Scrapbook* is a tribute to two men whose comedic art has endured for half a century.

—JACK SCAGNETTI

I.

Arthur Stanley Jefferson

Stan Laurel was born Arthur Stanley Jefferson on June 16, 1890, in Ulverston County, Lancaster, England. Stan's mother, Margaret Metcalfe Jefferson, had performed as an actress under the name of Madge Metcalf. His father, Arthur Jefferson, was a prominent comedian and sketch writer of the day. Stan had two brothers and a sister. His brother, Gordon, and sister, Olga, were both theater enthusiasts, Gordon eventually becoming a theater manager, and Olga an actress until she retired from the stage to get married. Stan's second brother, Teddy, was not interested in show business at all. He later became Stan's chauffeur.

Bitten by the theatrical bug at age nine, Stan persuaded his father to convert the attic of their home in North Shields into a small theater with a seating capacity of 30. With assistance from neighborhood boys and girls, Stan attended to the many managerial duties. Admission to the theater could be gained either by paying cash or by donating items which could be used as stage props. The theater operated smoothly with but one mishap: while one of the plays was being performed, the family home almost burned to the ground. During a scuffle in which Stan was struggling with the play's villain, one of the paraffin oil lamp footlights was knocked over; the side curtains quickly caught fire. As 30 guests fled the attic theater Stan's father arrived just in time to douse the flames with a chemical fire extinguisher. Despite this near tragedy, the theater soon resumed normal operations.

When Mr. Jefferson signed a long lease on the Metropole Theater in Glasgow in 1905, the family moved to Scotland. Stan attended Ruther Glen School and, later, Queen's Park Academy. Never fond of school, he played hookey often enough to convince his father that it would be a waste of time for him to continue. The elder Jefferson hoped to groom his son to become assistant manager and,

13

CERTIFIED COPY OF AN ENTRY OF BIRTH

GIVEN AT THE GENERAL REGISTER OFFICE,
SOMERSET HOUSE, LONDON.

Application Number......*C/677/72*......

REGISTRATION DISTRICT   *Ulverston*

1890.   BIRTH in the Sub-district of _____*Ulverston*_____ in the *County of Lancaster*

Columns:—	1	2	3	4	5	6	7	8	9	10*
No.	When and where born	Name, if any	Sex	Name, and surname of father	Name, surname, and maiden surname of mother	Occupation of father	Signature, description, and residence of informant	When registered	Signature of registrar	Name entered after registration
376	Sixteenth June 1890 Foundry Cottages Ulverston U.S.D.	Arthur Stanley	Boy	Arthur Jefferson	Margaret Jefferson formerly Metcalfe	Comedian	M. Jefferson Mother Foundry Cottages Ulverston	Eleventh July 1890	James Riley Registrar	—

CERTIFIED to be a true copy of an entry in the certified copy of a Register of Births in the District above mentioned.

Given at the GENERAL REGISTER OFFICE, SOMERSET HOUSE, LONDON, under the Seal of the said Office, the *12th* day of *September* 19*72*

*See note overleaf

BC 781846

This certificate is issued in pursuance of the Births and Deaths Registration Act 1953.
Section 34 provides that any certified copy of an entry purporting to be sealed or stamped with the seal of the General Register Office shall be received as evidence of the birth or death to which it relates without any further or other proof of the entry, and no certified copy purporting to have been given in the said Office shall be of any force or effect unless it is sealed or stamped as aforesaid.
CAUTION:—Any person who (1) falsifies any of the particulars on this certificate, or (2) uses a falsified certificate as true, knowing it to be false, is liable to prosecution.

Stan Laurel, as shown in this certified copy of his birth certificate, was born Arthur Stanley Jefferson on June 16, 1890.

eventually, manager, and he assigned him to various business duties at the Metropole.

But Stan had other ideas. He wanted to *perform* and was not interested in the myriad behind-the-scenes details. He was interested in comedy. Having made a successful debut as a comic at the Pickard Music Hall in Glasgow at age 16, Stan wanted desperately to return to the stage. He was thrilled by the laughter, applause and demands for an encore with which he had been greeted at the Pickard. Once, as he returned to the Music Hall stage for an encore, he dropped his silk topper hat and, as it rolled toward the footlights with him in pursuit, he accidentally kicked it into the orchestra pit. One of the pit musicians, in trying to retrieve the hat, inadvertently stepped on it and thoroughly squashed it. Dashing to the exit, Stan caught his frock coat on a steel hook attached to the stage's wings; the coat's skirt ripped apart and the audience howled.

Stan's father had witnessed his son's Music Hall performance and was impressed. He promised to help him obtain comedy work. But Arthur Jefferson's theater produced only melodramas, so, in 1907, he secured a booking for his son, then 17, with Levy and Cardwell's Juvenile Pantomimes, a company of youngsters aged six to 18. Levy and Cardwell staged satirical shows and clean burlesque shows. Stan remained with the company for two seasons playing comedy parts, and eventually became assistant stage manager. When the show closed after the second season, Stan, then 19, wrote a new single act for himself and went into vaudeville. He performed mostly in small English variety houses.

Later, he replaced one of the comedians in a successful vaudeville sketch, *Home from the Honeymoon,* produced by his father at major Scotland theaters. Edwin Marris, a noted musical comedy producer, cast him as a stableboy in *Gentleman Jockey,* a hit production, and he followed this with a contract as a comedian in *Alone in the World,* a melodrama.

Returning to vaudeville late in 1909 as a single act, Stan was spotted in Manchester, England by Fred Karno, a famous comedy producer whose music hall troupe featured Charlie Chaplin. Stan joined the company and was cast in *Jimmy the Fearless,* in which Chaplin was the star.

After nearly a week of rehearsal, Chaplin informed Karno that he didn't like the show and would not continue in it. Karno selected Stan as Chaplin's replacement. After two days of rehearsal in the new role, Stan opened in London. The show was a smash hit. Chaplin watched one week of performances and decided that he wanted the part after all. Chaplin was rehired and Stan remained with the company as second comedian. He went on to understudy Chaplin in 10 other Karno shows.

The troupe, billed as "Fred Karno's Comedians," was booked to play in America in 1910. Stan, then 20 years old, set sail with the group for the United States. The Karno troupe was scheduled to tour the Sullivan and Considine vaudeville circuit across the United States, with Chaplin as the lead comedian in a satire entitled *A Night in an English Music Hall.* When Stan was refused a salary increase, he left the company and returned to England. Home again, he wrote a sketch called *The Rum 'Uns from Rome,* which he performed with various partners in England and on the Continent.

When the Karno company was again booked to tour the United States in 1912, Stan rejoined the troupe as Chaplin's understudy—at the salary which he had earlier requested. During this tour, in 1913, Chaplin was signed by Mack Sennett to make comedy films in Hollywood at $125 per week, $50 more than he was earning with Karno. This offered Stan the opportunity of playing the leading role (of a drunk) in the company.

But, when the company reached Philadelphia, there was trouble: Karno had signed a 12-week contract with the Nixon-Nirdlinger circuit, which specified that Chaplin was to star in the shows. The Nixon-Nirdlinger people, upon learning that Chaplin was no longer a member of the company, refused to accept the show with Stan Laurel in the lead—this, despite the fact that Karno's manager advised them that Stan was every bit as good as Chaplin. They would allow the shows to be performed only if Karno brought a comic named Dan Raynor over from England. Raynor, the top comedian from the London-based Karno company, made the trip to the United States, but the show played only a couple of weeks. It was a flop. The balance of the contract was canceled and the group was disbanded in 1913.

Stan was offered a ticket back to England, but decided to remain in the United States and seek work on his own. He was able to get a day's work in a vaudeville house doing a shadowgraph act (before a white screen) in which he portrayed a drunk in a cafe.

By now, audiences were beginning to recognize Stan Laurel's extraordinary ability as a mimic; he was a keen student and had great insight into human behavior. Stan proved that without words, songs or tricks he could make people laugh.

Together with two other members of the disbanded Karno group, Edgar Hurley and his wife, Stan decided to produce an act called The Nutty Burglars. It opened in Chicago and played the Midwest for several months. The act, although not very lengthy, attracted the attention of Gordon Bostock, a booking agent. Bostock rewrote it and changed its name to The Keystone Trio. In it Stan played a tramp character, similar to the one played by Charlie Chaplin in the Keystone Comedies, which were now becoming popular. Mr. and Mrs. Hurley played characters similar to Chester Conklin and Mabel Normand, also Keystone stars.

The new characterizations helped make the act a great success, and when Hurley expressed his desire to play the tramp role, a dispute arose between him and Laurel. Hurley copyrighted the act—without informing Stan—and, claiming that he owned all rights to the material, replaced Stan with another actor. When theater managers discovered that Stan was no longer one of The Keystone Trio, bookings became difficult to come by and the act soon disbanded.

Stan now decided to form a group to be known as The Stan Jefferson Trio, and which was to include Alice Hamilton and her husband, Baldwin Cooke. Stan wrote an act for them in the summer of 1916, and changed the group's name to The Crazy Cracksman, a laugh riot full of crazy gags. They were paid $175 per week, to be divided equally among the three. The trio rented a cottage near the Atlantic Highlands in New Jersey, holding daily rehearsals and passing their leisure enjoying food, drink and good times. They spent their salaries as soon as they received them. Typical of vaudeville performers in 1916, they lived for the moment. Those were happy-go-lucky days for Stan.

In 1918, in a small Pennsylvania town, Stan met Mae Charlotte Dahlberg, a beautiful Australian singer/dancer who performed in a dancing sister act which appeared on the same bill with him. Stan became interested in Mae, who was two years his senior. Before long, he left The Crazy Cracksman to create a new act with Mae. It was at this point that Stan changed his name. Stan Jefferson totaled 13 letters, and this was unlucky, he thought. He adopted the name of Stan Laurel, which he later legalized. Why did he choose Laurel as his new surname? Simply because he liked the sound of it!

The new comedy team was billed as Stan and Mae Laurel. The couple lived as common law husband and wife, and they toured the country. Stan continually added new gags to their routines and provided vaudeville fans with a full measure of laughs.

While playing the Hippodrome in Los Angeles early in 1917, Stan had so impressed the owner, Adolph Ramish, that he was now asked by Ramish to appear in a two-reel film (usually running 20 minutes long). Ramish, who considered Stan funnier than Chaplin, hired Bobby Williamson, a former comic, as director.

In this early photograph, Stan Laurel wears heavy make-up for a stage appearance on the vaudeville circuit.

Titled *Nuts in May,* the silent movie was shot in a small studio in the Boyle Heights area of Los Angeles. When the film previewed at the Hippodrome, Ramish invited Charlie Chaplin and Carl Laemmle, then head of Universal Studios, to see it. *Nuts in May* was the story of a man who, dressed in a business suit and a Napoleon hat, escaped from an insane asylum. Laurel's pantomime performance reminded the audience very much of Chaplin.

After the preview, Stan and Chaplin talked over dinner, Chaplin complimenting Stan on his performance and revealing that he was planning to leave

Mutual, the studio with which he was then associated, in order to launch a studio of his own. He would film his own comedies. Chaplin also explained that he planned to form a stock company of screen comedians who would produce separate films and he suggested that Stan join the group.

Carl Laemmle was also very much impressed by *Nuts in May*. When he met with Stan, he invited him to work for Universal.

Stan pondered what to do. He decided to wait for a stronger commitment from Chaplin, but when several weeks had passed and Chaplin still had not contacted him, Stan signed a one-year contract with Laemmle to do comedy films at Universal.

Stan Laurel proceeded to play a character known as Hickory Hiram in three or four comedies by the same name. He was far from impressed by the caliber of the material. Luckily for him, and quite coincidentally, Universal was undergoing a period of reorganization at the time and all contracts were canceled without notice, leaving Stan once again a free agent.

Stan immediately returned to the vaudeville circuit, and Mae Dahlberg, who had appeared with him in the *Hickory Hiram* comedies, continued on as his partner. Laurel returned to Hollywood a number of times in 1918 to make five one-reel comedies for Hal Roach. These films were written to star Toto, the famous clown, but Toto quit in the middle of shooting to return to the tent hippodrome circuit. Stan replaced him.

In that same year, Stan also shot a two-reel pilot film for G.M. "Bronco Billy" Anderson, one of the first Hollywood cowboy stars to become a comedy producer. In the film, *Lucky Dog,* Stan enters a stray dog in a dog show and wins first prize. When the owners appear, he is accused of stealing the dog, but is eventually exonerated. In one scene, as he hurries down a street, Laurel is held up by a masked bandit. The small bandit part was played by Oliver (Babe) Hardy.

Laurel and Hardy were on friendly terms, but their relationship was of no special significance. Upon the completion of *Lucky Dog,* Stan returned to vaudeville, and Hardy continued to work for various studios, invariably being cast as a villain.

Stan's vaudeville career was again interrupted in 1919 when he was hired by Vitagraph Pictures to appear in a film with comedy star Larry Semon.

Semon, aware that Stan possessed comic ability equal to his own, did his utmost to prevent Laurel from "stealing" scenes. In *Scars and Stripes,* Semon insisted on rewriting a chase scene so that he, himself, would be featured. In the scene, he had Stan handcuffed and tied to a tree so that he could do the chase footage. Although Vitagraph was paying Stan $10 a day, respectable wages in 1919, he decided never to work with Semon again.

From late 1918 through the early 1920s, Stan and Mae, still living together, maintained a hectic schedule of vaudeville appearances in the Midwest, Canada, the Pacific Northwest, southern California, Texas, Montana and other western states and major eastern cities. Stan and Mae enjoyed a very close relationship, but marriage was out of the question at that time since Mae had a husband living in Australia who was not interested in a divorce. So Stan and Mae continued their life as a common law couple. And although their relationship was not without its bitter quarrels, many of these outbursts taking place in their dressing room before or after a performance, Mae's sense of humor brought great joy to Stan.

In 1922, Stan Laurel returned to Hollywood to work once again with G.M. "Bronco Billy" Anderson on several two-reel parodies of feature films of the era. One of the most clever was *Mud and Sand,* a spoof on the then-current and popular *Blood and Sand* which starred Rudolph Valentino. Stan played Rhubarb Vaselino, a Latin lover and bullfighter. In one hilarious scene in *Mud and Sand,* Stan bids goodbye to his native village to seek his fortune in the big city. As he does so, he falls off the horse and into a mud puddle. Another of the parodies, *When Knights Were Cold* (a spoof on Douglas Fairbanks' *Robin Hood*) includes a hilarious chase sequence.

Although the Anderson comedies were well done, financing could not be found for future film projects. Again, Stan returned to vaudeville, only to be summoned back to Hollywood in 1923 to make a series of comedy films for Hal Roach: 12 one-reelers and 12 two-reelers.

Roach, a native of Elmira, New York, had entered the movie business as a $5-a-day cowboy in 1912, and four years later was producing films at age 22. He had inherited $3,000, and with it made a one-reel comedy, *Just Nuts,* with Harold Lloyd in the lead. Roach and Lloyd made several other films together before Lloyd left to work with Mack Sennett and The Keystone Comedies. From 1923 to 1926, Roach made a number of one- and two-reel slapstick shorts under the banner of *Comedy All-Stars,* and they soon became serious rivals to the Mack Sennett comedies. He sought a Chaplin or a Buster Keaton-type comedian; none of the comedians who were already working for him, including Ben Turpin, Snub Pollard, Billy Bevan and Charlie Chase quite fit the bill. Continuing the search, Roach remembered the fine job Stan Laurel had done in the five one-reelers he made in 1918, and recalled his impressive performance in Anderson's *Mud and Sand.* Roach offered the role to Laurel, and he readily accepted.

The one- and two-reelers produced by Roach in the early 1920s were mostly spoofs: *Under Two Jags,* a take-off on *Under Two Flags; The Soilers,* a parody of the Rex Beach adventure called *The Spoilers; Rupert of Cole Slaw* (Hentzau), and *Wild Bill Hiccup* (Hickok). Mae's insistence that she appear with Stan in the Roach comedies is reported to have caused conflict between the comedian and Roach. Pathe, then distributing Roach's comedies, took a dim view of the suggestion that Mae be a part of the Laurel comedies. Added to this, reports of Stan having a drinking problem further weakened the Roach/Laurel relationship.

When his work with Roach was completed in late 1924, Stan signed a contract with comedian Joe Rock, formerly of Vitagraph Studios, to star in a new series of comedies. Rock, a former stunt man and a newcomer to producing, had some good ideas. He proposed that Stan star in 12 comedies, at a larger salary

Joe Rock, pictured here, produced 12 comedies starring Stan Laurel in 1925 and 1926. Stan left Rock's studio in 1926 to work for Hal Roach.

than the comedian had ever made. (Rock, to this day, has refused to reveal Laurel's exact salary.) Also, Stan was to receive 15% of the profit from each film. Being in desperate financial straits at the time, the film contract with Rock was most welcome.

"He had patches in the seat of his pants and had to pull his coattail down to cover them when he stood up," said Joe Rock. "He had cardboard in his shoes to cover the holes in them. He admitted that he had never been lower in his life. I gave him $1,000 to buy clothes and food for himself and Mae, and then I left Hollywood for New York to sound out distributors on buying a Stan Laurel series."

In New York, distributors expressed skepticism that Stan Laurel would be able to complete the project. They feared that his much-talked-about drinking problem, (probably the result of his troubles with Mae), would interfere with his work. Stan would be working on something he loved, Rock explained by way of countering the skeptics. He would succeed in completing the project. But the distributors remained unconvinced; they refused to sign a contract with Rock for the Laurel comedies. Rock returned to Hollywood and decided to proceed with the films despite the lack of distributor interest.

A day before shooting of the first picture was to begin Stan met with Joe Rock. When Laurel entered Rock's office, the producer noticed three or four deep scratches on the comic's face. Unable to convince Joe that a cat had scratched him, Stan finally admitted that he had been bruised during a heated argument with Mae in which she insisted that she also appear in the picture. Rock refused to engage her, forcing Stan to present him with an ultimatum: if Mae couldn't work in the film, he wouldn't either. Rock retorted that at least six comedians were prepared to take his place at a moment's notice. Stan calmed down. When Rock suggested that he talk to Mae personally, Stan consented. Standing face-to-face with Mae, Rock later made it clear that he would find a replacement for Stan if she insisted on appearing in the film. She finally abandoned her demand, and production began.

About midway through the year's contract, it became evident that Stan was again being plagued by personal difficulties. He repeatedly showed up late on the set, looking haggard. He seemed to be drinking more than usual, was impatient with his fellow workers, and disliked having to reshoot scenes. Again, the cause of the difficulty was Mae. According to Rock, she was pressuring Stan to return to vaudeville. Moreover, she was reportedly disenchanted with America, and would return to her native Australia if she could find the money.

Rock arranged for Mae to return to Autralia. Not only did he agree to pay her fare, but he redeemed her jewels from a pawn shop, and he gave her two hundred dollars in cash. The total cost to Rock was about $1,000, which, he figured, was a worthwhile investment. Mae had, after all, been a stone around Stan's neck for years.

Other than having to deal with the problems posed by Mae, Joe Rock had another problem: his distributor, Lewis J. Selznick, father of David O. Selznick and Myron Selznick, was in serious financial straits after distributing 1,050 prints of Rock's seven Laurel films and three Jim Aubrey comedies throughout the country. Rock rushed to New York in order to obtain a court order that would force Selznick to relinquish all distribution rights. The court order granted, Rock arranged for the comedies to be handled by Film Booking Office (FBO).

Joe Rock was still concerned about Laurel. He feared that Stan might sink into a severe depression after Mae's departure for Australia. To counteract this eventuality, he arranged to have his brother, Murray, move in with Stan, hoping that Murray would help keep Stan's mind off his troubles.

Rock then arranged to have Stan meet Lois Neilson, a beautiful blonde in-genue with whom Rock had worked at Vitagraph and who was a friend of Rock's wife, Louise. Joe's hope was that Stan would be swept off his feet by the blonde beauty. The first meeting between Stan and Lois took place in the early spring of 1926 when Mae was well on her way to Australia. At first sight, Stan and Lois fell in love. Shortly thereafter, on August 23, 1926 (a significant date in Hollywood's movie history—Rudolph Valentino, the screen's immortal lover, died that day), Stan Laurel and Lois Neilson were married.

The films that Joe Rock had made with Stan Laurel were two-reelers, simply called the *Stan Laurel Comedies.* They had been filmed in studio space which Joe had rented from Universal. As part of the deal, he was granted the right to use any of the old sets on the premises that were still in good condition. A beautiful set was used for *Monsieur Don't Care,* a spoof of Valentino's *Monsieur Beaucaire.* An elaborate set that had been built for the *Hunchback of Notre Dame,* starring Lon Chaney, was used for *Dr. Pyckle and Mr. Pryde,* a comedy which contains a delightful scene in which Stan aims a peashooter at unaware pedestrians on London streets.

For his performance in one of Rock's funniest productions, *Half a Man,* Stan was hailed by critics who called him a combination of Charlie Chaplin and Harry Langdon. The two-reeler was shot on location in the summer of 1925 at beautiful Catalina Island off the southern California coast. Laurel played the innocent and lovable Winchell McSweeney, a scion of a fishing family. When informed by his mother of the bad news that, because family finances were so low, he would have to go out and make his own living, he sobs and licks his lollipop. Later, after foolishly becoming entangled on the beach in a suspended fishing net, McSweeney boards a small boat which is about to leave the dock. On board, he discovers dozens of beautiful girls, but flees from them when he recalls his mother's warning about girls. An Amazon succeeds in capturing poor Winchell, carries him to a table, ties a napkin around his neck and spoonfeeds him. While eating, the motion of the ship causes him to get seasick and he rushes to the railing for relief.

Later, Winchell accidentally sets the boat afire and, in an attempt to save his life, puts on every life jacket he can find. All the girls escape in a lifeboat, while the male sailors leap overboard. In a brilliant mime sequence, Stan, alone on the boat, and terrified of jumping, prays heavenward.

The next scene takes place on a deserted island where the girls have arrived safely. Seeing soggy Stan walking along the beach, they chase after him until he reaches a cliff high above the sea. He threatens to jump if they don't leave him alone, and the girls plead with him not to. At that very moment, they spot the other male members of the crew reaching the island. The film ends with the Amazon hurling Stan overboard and being caught by another girl from the boat. As they skip along the beach happily together, "The End" is flashed on the screen.

True, *Half a Man* had a very simple, almost childish, plot. But Stan's gift at pantomime and improvisation made the movie a delight. Had his career developed differently, Stan might very likely have developed an interesting solo character to rival the likes of Chaplin and Langdon.

Murray Rock, brother of producer Joe Rock, offers seasick Stan Laurel some food in a scene from Half a Man.

Stan, in his pre-Laurel and Hardy days, plays a scene with Jimmy Finlayson. Finlayson later appeared in several of the team's pictures.

Laurel spent several weeks filming each of the 12 two-reelers he made with Rock during the first year of the contract. He enjoyed the work immensely.

"We always had some idea of a story line and many gags thought out before the shooting began," said Rock. But Stan was always on the set early, and continued working with the writers at all hours of the day or night.

After the success of *Half a Man*, released in August, 1925, Rock told Stan that he wanted to use Oliver (Babe) Hardy in some of the Stan Laurel comedies. Stan's refusal was understandable; no leading comedy star wanted to team with another comic—that is, unless that comic was playing the stooge, straight man or foil. Rock felt that Stan's refusal to team up with Hardy was not due to any dislike of Oliver, but, rather out of Laurel's awareness that in the Semon comedies Hardy had been quite adept at stealing scenes.

Stan's success in the Rock films brought him offers from many studios. In the last half-year of his contract with Rock, Stan was earning $1,000 per film plus 15% of the film's profits. At that time, no comic other than Chaplin and Harold Lloyd, producers of their own comedies, shared in profits.

Stan finished his 12 films with Rock three months before the expiration date of the first year's contract. Knowing Rock relied on the distributor's monies, and was therefore limited in the amount he would be able to pay, Laurel did not seek to renew his contract. He was immediately hired by Hal Roach to write a scenario for a pilot one-reel film starring Jimmy Finlayson.

In moving to the Hal Roach Studios while still under contract to Rock, Stan became involved in legal problems. Rock, learning that Stan was writing, directing and possibly acting at Roach while still technically under contract to him, was placed in an embarrassing situation with his distributor who was expecting to get more Laurel comedies. Rock's contract with Stan had called for an option to make 12 pictures a year for four more years, during which time Stan was not to appear in films for any other studios.

Stan's lawyers advised him to sue Rock for $250,000 for depriving him of making a living if Rock insisted on the four-year option. Rock countered with a breach of contract action. Lawyers for both sides met and a settlement was reached: Stan was permitted to work for Roach, but he had to forego his percentage of profits on the films he had made with Rock.

A proud father, Stan holds his only daughter, Lois, born in 1927.

The loss to Joe Rock of a comedian of Stan Laurel's stature was considerable but did not prevent him from achieving success. He went on to make 24 two-reel films with Jimmy Aubrey and 24 two-reelers with The Three Fat Men, sometimes known as "A Ton of Fun"—Frank (Fatty) Alexander, Fat Karr and Kewpie Ross. He also made a series of 12 comedies called *Blue Ribbon*, featuring Alice Ardell and supported by such comedians as Chester Conklin and Slim Summerville. He later produced 20 feature films, and in 1933 received an Oscar from the Academy of Motion Picture Arts and Sciences for his documentary film, *Krakatoa*.

Laurel's work in 1926 as a writer and gag man for Roach found him involved with crafty comedians that included Ben Turpin, Charley Chase, Edgar Kennedy, James Finlayson, Billy Gilbert, Billy Bevan, the Our Gang Comedy Kids, Snub Pollard and Oliver Hardy. They were billed as the Comedy All-Stars and recognized as a very talented and versatile group. Stan joined in the numerous gag sessions the group held to plot comedies, and his ideas were welcomed. They frequently worked overtime, but no one minded. All members of the group loved their work.

Roach was not anxious to let Stan act very much in films because he felt that Stan's very pale blue eyes did not photograph well. When panchromatic films were beginning to be used, however, Roach gave Stan a screen test and found that there was no longer a problem.

The studio's Dick Jones was responsible for Stan's return to acting. Assigned to direct a comedy called *Get 'Em Young,* Stan was persuaded by Jones to replace Oliver Hardy, who had been seriously burned when he spilled some hot gravy on himself. Jones was unable to hire another comedian on such short notice, and Stan at first refused. But when offered a $100 raise, he agreed to play the whimpering butler that was to have been played by Hardy. It was in this film that he developed the mannerism of crying and distorting his face, a characterestic that was to become a Laurel trademark in future years.

Stan made *Get 'Em Young,* and, in the process, discovered that he favored writing and directing over acting. He had already successfully directed a few Roach comedies, and he decided to do some more writing. Roach agreed and assigned him to write a film, *Slipping Wives,* for Priscilla Dean, Herbert Rawlinson and Albert Conti. Jones asked him to write a part for himself into the picture. Again Stan refused, but when Roach offered him an additional $100 raise, he agreed.

Stan wrote the scenario for *Slipping Wives,* a story about an artist, his beautiful wife, a comic butler, and a paint salesman. The butler and paint salesman would be played by Stan Laurel and Oliver Hardy.

2.

Oliver Norvell Hardy

Little is known about Oliver Hardy's younger days. He was never one to talk much of his past.

Born in Harlem (near Augusta), Georgia, on January 18, 1892, Oliver Norvell Hardy was the son of Oliver Hardy, a big, heavy-set man of English stock. His mother, Emily Norvell, was a heavily-built woman of Scottish descent. It came as no surprise when baby Oliver was born weighing a striking 14 pounds.

Unlike Stan's parents, Oliver Hardy's were not in show business. His father was a lawyer who died when the future comedian was only 18 months old. Upon his death, Oliver's mother moved the entire family to Madison. Several years later they moved to Milledgeville, near Macon, Georgia, where Emily Hardy operated the Baldwin Hotel.

While growing up at the hotel, Oliver developed a habit that he was to retain throughout his life: he watched and studied people. He enjoyed sitting in the lobby and observing people—their movements, their mannerisms. What he learned about people in these early years served him well in the future when called upon to portray a wide variety of characters.

The entire Hardy family, including Oliver's two stepbrothers, and two half-sisters of Emily's former marriage, loved music and the theater. They especially enjoyed singing—and Oliver, the youngest of the five children, was encouraged by every member of the family to sing along.

Oliver also loved the theater. He was fascinated by theatrical people who stayed at the Baldwin and often related show business stories. His interest in the theater continued to grow and, at the age of eight, he "ran away" from home to join Coburn's Minstrels, a troupe traveling through the south. As a boy soprano in the show, he sang two hit songs, "Silver Threads Among the Gold" and "When

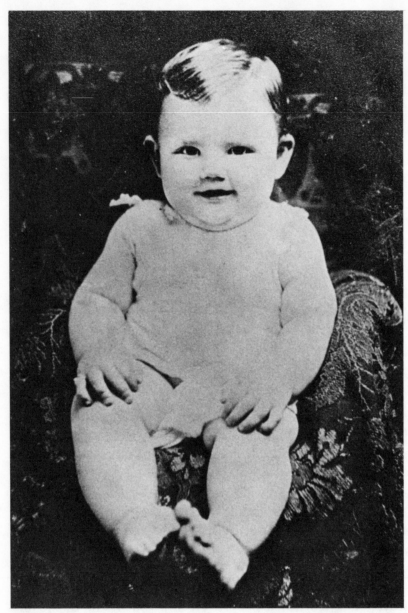

As this photograph, taken at the age of nine months, shows, Oliver Hardy was a big baby. He weighed 14 pounds at birth.

You and I Were Young, Maggie." Emily Hardy always knew of her son's whereabouts and she was assured by the show's owner, Charles Coburn, a personal friend, that he would look after the youngster.

When Coburn's Minstrels went on tour, young Oliver joined them. But he soon became homesick for his family and, after a few months, returned to Milledgeville. Though he was happy to be home, Oliver couldn't get show business out of his blood, and he soon began attending theater performances in Atlanta. When he started to neglect his school studies, Mrs. Hardy became concerned and enrolled him in a Milledgeville boarding school.

When one of the elder Hardy boys suffered a broken neck in a swimming pool accident one summer, Oliver, age 12, and a friend, pulled him from the water. The boy died. The experience was traumatic for Oliver; he would never forget it.

Oliver Hardy continued to detest school. His first love was the stage (he had been singing to slides at a local theater) and, on April 17, 1906, he took off for Atlanta. On the day of his arrival a violent race riot erupted in Atlanta, and 14-year-old Oliver was innocently caught in the midst of it. He was pushed and bandied about; and his clothes were covered with red mud. He finally found refuge in the Atlanta railroad station.

A kindly stationmaster helped the youngster clean up. He telephoned Oliver's mother who quickly came after him. When Oliver refused to return to boarding school, Mrs. Hardy permitted him to stay in Atlanta, 80 miles from Milledgeville, with her sister, Susie. Oliver was ecstatic, and lost no time in registering to study voice at the Atlanta Conservatory of Music under Adolph Daym Peterson, one of the best musicians in the south.

After several weeks, Mrs. Hardy traveled to Atlanta to visit her son. She discovered that he hadn't attended his music classes for a week. Instead, she found him working in a movie house, singing to illustrated slides for 50 cents a day. This infuriated her and she insisted that Oliver return to Milledgeville, granting him permission to sing only on Saturdays and holidays.

Oliver was registered in the Georgia Military Academy, a government-supervised military school in Milledgeville. On one occasion, he ran away from the academy claiming that he wasn't fed enough. There may have been an element of truth to his claim: although he was only 14, he weighed 250 pounds. Once, his mother made him 20 baking powder biscuits which he ate at one sitting. Oliver's classmates made fun of his size, and this upset him greatly. But Oliver was no slouch; he was quite adept at returning insults to those from whose mouths they came.

At the academy, Oliver showed evidence of possessing a good deal of stage presence and personality. When undergraduates staged a skit called *Who Killed Cock Robin?*, he walked on stage in his costume and sang in a beautiful tenor voice:

I killed Cock Robin!
I tolled the bell,
because I could pull the rope.
I am the bull!
The audience roared with laughter.

Oliver also brought forth laughs from classmates at the academy when, during exercise drill periods, he would get so tired that he would lie flat on the ground to rest. No matter how hard they tried, nobody could get him to move.

Oliver was active in sports, particularly baseball and football, and was frequently asked to umpire local baseball games. As an umpire, he always put on a good show. He would become irate, however, if the crowd started calling him "Fatty" or "Fats," threatening to leave the playing field if they didn't stop the name-calling.

Upon completion of his studies at Georgia Military Academy, Oliver expressed a desire to become a lawyer like his father. The Hardy family didn't take him too seriously, but Oliver's desire to follow in his father's footsteps grew stronger. If he became a lawyer, he reasoned, he would be of great financial help to his mother.

At the age of 18, Hardy entered the University of Georgia to study law. While a student there, he and three classmates formed a musical group called Half-a-Ton of Harmony, a quartet in which he played the drums. They performed in and around Atlanta on weekends and during vacation.

Oliver remained in college only briefly. He preferred show business as a career, and decided to make a musical tour of the south, playing cabarets, clubs, and state fairs; he even worked as an "end man" in a minstrel show for a short time. He sang in motion picture houses and night clubs, hung around theaters, hotel lobbies, lunch counters, cabarets, pool rooms and restaurants. Wherever someone associated with the theatrical profession could be found, no matter how remote that connection, Hardy would gravitate.

Oliver managed to save enough money to go to Atlanta. He loved the legitimate theater, and the closest one to him was in Atlanta. When, on one occasion, he heard singer Enrico Caruso perform in a theater in Atlanta, he was thrilled. Caruso's voice was the greatest he had ever been privileged to hear, and the experience so inspired him that he made up his mind to become a singer. In later years, Hardy often recalled this period in his life.

In 1910, when he was 18, Oliver went to work as manager of the first movie house to open in Milledgeville. He ran the theater for three years, serving also as its projectionist. Viewing the early silent comedies day after day, he thought to himself that he could do as well, or even better than most of the comics on the screen. He left his theater job in 1913, and traveled to Jacksonville, Florida, where he knew many films were being made.

In Jacksonville, Hardy got a job singing in a cabaret at night. He spent his days looking for film work, and finally landed a part-time job at $5 a week with Lubin Motion Pictures.

Oliver enjoyed the film work so much that he reported to the set even on days that he wasn't scheduled to work. He wanted to watch and learn, and was eager to help others on the set—the carpenters, painters and electricians. Everyone was impressed by him and he was soon guaranteed at least three days work a week at a salary of $5 per day.

Film production in 1913 was quite different from what it is today: the cast helped the production crew in arranging sets, while members of the crew would often serve as extras if needed. Consequently, Hardy was able to learn a great deal about the motion picture business. On occasion, he was called upon to work as an assistant cameraman, a script clerk, an assistant director and, in an acute emergency, even as a director.

It was in Jacksonville that he first acquired the nickname "Babe." He patronized a barber shop near the studio, and whenever the barber, who had a thick Italian accent, would finish shaving him, he would pat powder on his face, and say, "nice baby." Fellow workers kidded him about it and started to call him

"Baby," and then "Babe." The pet name was to stay with him for the rest of his life.

Babe started to play bit parts in Jacksonville and eventually became a full-time member of Lubin's stock companies. (Film studios in those days maintained groups of available actors, similar to the legitimate theater.) Most of the roles assigned to Hardy were villains. His excessive weight and massive 6-foot-1 frame made him the ideal "heavy."

Hardy (center) played tackle for the Lubin studio team. The team here poses for a victory photograph after beating its arch rival, Kalem, by a score of 8-0 in 1914.

In 1915, Babe made a film with Lubin which would, in later years, appear to be the prototype of a typical Laurel and Hardy film. Called *The Paper Hanger's Helper,* the film saw him co-star with Bobby Ray, a thin, short man, who, while he didn't look like Stan Laurel, was like him in many ways. Ray played Babe's helper and was the "fall guy"; Hardy was the "wise man."

This rare photograph, taken in 1913 or 1914, shows Hardy dressed as a woman for a film role with Lubin Motion Pictures.

Despite his full-time work in films, Hardy continued to sing evenings in cabarets. Singing continued to be his first love, and to become a vocalist was his foremost ambition. His repertoire consisted mostly of romantic ballads suited to his tenor voice and typical of the day.

At about this time Hardy was placed in charge of entertainment at the Burbridge Hotel and Cabaret, a high-class Jacksonville night spot. He now had money in his pocket for the first time, and he purchased his first automobile. At about this same time, Hardy joined the Masonic Order's Solomon Lodge No. 20. This affiliation greatly influenced his thinking, and he underook to live up to Masonic ideals—goodness, honesty and the teachings of the Bible.

Babe had always been a person of good character. He was thoughtful about his future, and he took his work seriously. In fact, he took all things in life seriously. He showed concern not only for his mother and her welfare, but was extraordinarily sensitive to the needs of others. His friends considered him generous, sympathetic, helpful and very sentimental. His affiliation with the Masonic Order, and his devotion to its principles strengthened these affirmative qualities which ruled Hardy's life.

When, after three years, Vim Studios assumed control of the Lubin enterprise, Oliver Hardy became the star comic. In one comedy, he played a villain dressed in women's clothes, and his performance was received very favorably.

In 1917, the 25-year-old Hardy felt ambitious and ready to try his luck at the big time. Hardy traveled to New York to line up free-lance work with various film companies, including Pathe, Gaumont, Wharton, Edison and Vitagraph.

During those early film days in New York, he worked in a series with comedian Harry Meyers and his comedienne wife, Rosemary Phoebe. He also played in a series called *Pump and Runt*. But Hardy was frustrated and disappointed in New York, for the cold weather and the metropolitan hustle and bustle were alien to him, and not to his liking. He found himself spending considerable time commuting from his Brooklyn rooming house to the film studios scattered in the various suburbs, with little time left to pursue his singing career. Moreover, he discovered that singers in New York were not only plentiful, but were superior to those in the south—which meant that the competition was keener. To make matters worse, Hardy now found himself very low on funds.

In April of 1917, the United States entered World War I and Babe decided to enlist in the military service. He walked into a recruiting office and announced his intentions. The two Army men in charge looked at his enormous size and reacted with laughter. Then they added several tasteless remarks which Hardy did not find the least bit funny. Terribly embarrassed and his feelings hurt, Babe left the recruiting office and the City of New York and returned to Jacksonville where he went to work for Vim.

Back in Jacksonville, Hardy made several one-reel comedies. But a few months later, when the stock company began to scatter, he went back to New York. Luck was with him this time: he was hired to play the villain in The Billy West Comedies. As the foremost Chaplin imitator, West was very popular in those days. Typical of the heavies of the era, Babe donned a heavy beard and bushy eyebrows.

In December of 1918, Hardy moved to California to seek his fortune in Hollywood, which was at that time quickly establishing itself as the nation's film capital. World War I had just ended and the film industry was on the verge of a boom. Work was available for exprienced performers.

In Hollywood, Babe again worked for Billy West Comedies. Coincidentally, the studio's director, Arvid Gilstrom, had moved to California at about the same time as Hardy. Babe also worked in a series of films for Hollywood's King Bee Studios. In 1919, he played in a picture series at L-KO Studios and made three films (again cast as a villain) for Vitagraph, starring Earl Williams. That same year, he appeared in two separate series of Jimmy Aubrey Comedies; in one series he played a villain, in the other the straight man. The series of 12 was directed by Knowles Smith, and the series of 10 was directed by Jesse Robins.

In 1920, Babe acted in several of cowboy star Buck Jones' early films directed by W. S. Van Dyke at William Fox's Western Avenue Studio. In these films, he usually played the heavy although occasionally he played other characters.

Hardy also made some two-reelers for Mack Sennett. He received $125 a week from 1921 to 1924 to play the "heavy" opposite Larry Semon at Vitagraph. Semon was one of filmdom's most popular comedians of the era. Among the Semon comedies in which Babe appeared were *The Perfect Clown,* and the 1925 version of *The Wizard of Oz.*

Hardy (with the gun) plays a villain in an early twenties film.

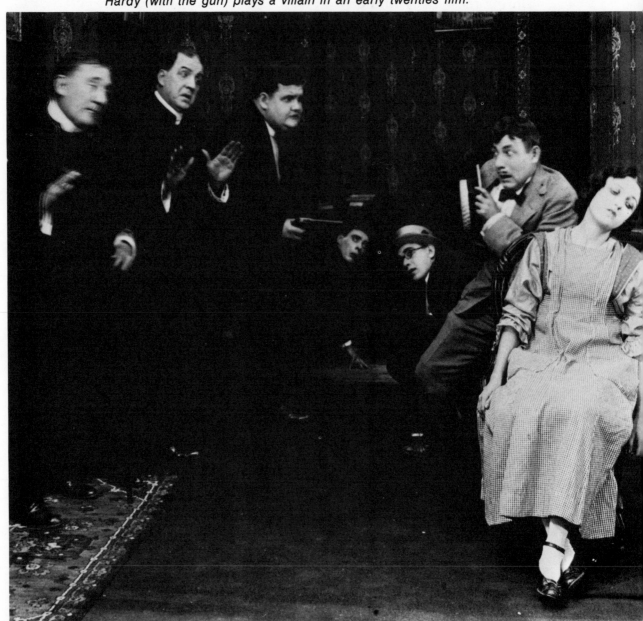

When playing villains, Hardy was made up to appear unshaven, with scarred face and black eyes. At times, he was dressed in sartorial splendor, a man whose elegant, dapper, polished behavior might be comically upset by his being dumped into a mud puddle or hit with a bucket of mush. However, Semon, who directed the films in which he appeared, feared that Hardy might overshadow him. Hardy could capture audience attention with a simple turn of the head, or by adjusting his derby or his tie. Semon saw to it that many of Babe's scenes were shot in medium or long shots, while his own were mostly close-ups.

One of the best films in the Semon series was *Kid Speed,* made in 1924, starring Semon and famous fighter James J. Corbett. Produced by Chadwick Pictures Corporation, it was described as a "fast and funny stunt comedy."

Oliver autographed this 1934 photograph to a friend, Monty. Few photographs from the 1930s show Hardy without a hat.

Hardy's distinguished profile and his ever-present derby are captured in this silhouette drawing by Arthur Forrester.

Later in 1924, Hal Roach Studios hired Hardy as a villain in a two-reeler, *Rex, King of the Wild Horses.* Although it helped establish Babe at Roach Studios, he had still not succeeded in attaining status as a solo comedian, despite more than 10 years of film experience. Roach was using him as a contract player in two-reel comedies, mostly in minor roles. He no longer was type cast as the villain, however, and no longer required the extensive make-up jobs that he once did. He now began to develop the comic character for which he was to become so famous, working at it persistently in order to perfect his mannerisms. These included staring directly at the audience, getting a bashful smile to spread slowly across an angelic face, and a variety of hand and foot gestures.

Babe later revealed that his screen character was one that grew gradually. The Ollie Hardy character, he explained, was partly based on a cartoon character called Helpful Henry, which had appeared in Georgia newspapers when he was growing up. The fussy Helpful Henry was always trying to be helpful, but invariably made a mess of everything. Helpful Henry wore a derby; but Hardy claimed that he had worn a derby since his early acting days in Florida.

At Roach, Babe played roles in which the script required that he *react* to situations rather than *instigate* them. Such was the case in comedies starring Charlie Chase, a famous comedian of the day. In *Fluttering Hearts,* Charlie, with the help of a sexy-looking store manikin, lures Hardy to the darkened corner of a speak-easy. In *Crazy Like a Fox,* Hardy performed pantomime reactions to a display of insanity by Charlie. And in another Chase comedy, *Long Fliv the King,* he played a general whose uniform is ruined by a scoop of ice cream.

In 1925, at the age of 33, Hardy married. His bride was Myrtle Lee Reeves, an actress, about whom little information is available. Whether or not Hardy had any serious love interests prior to Myrtle is a mystery. A shy, private person off camera, he kept his private life closed to public view.

Although Oliver Hardy had gained a good foothold in Hollywood by 1925, he was not yet a star. Destiny, however, found him working at the same studio as Stan Laurel—and that fact was soon to change his life.

3.

Teammates

Working at the same studio—the Hal Roach Studio—in 1926, it was inevitable that Stan Laurel and Oliver Hardy would appear in some of the same films. In 1927, in addition to *Slipping Wives,* they both appeared—although not as a team—in 13 films, including *Love 'Em and Weep, Sailors Beware, Why Girls Love Sailors, Love and Hisses, Sugar Daddies,* and *Should Tall Men Marry?* All were two-reelers made as part of the Comedy All Stars series, and Laurel and Hardy received the same billing as other Roach comedians. However, in each successive film they seemed to be more like a team, and, because the audiences responded to them so well, their parts began to grow larger and larger.

Leo McCarey, a production supervisor at Roach who sometimes directed films, is generally credited with forming the Laurel and Hardy team. He was the first to notice that placing thin Stan and fat Babe side by side was immediately laugh-provoking. McCarey directed the first official film featuring them as a team and called it a "Laurel and Hardy Comedy." The film, however, *Putting Pants on Phillip,* was not released until several months after completion. In the early years of filmmaking, films were not always released in the order in which they were produced.

The films that Roach had made before 1927 were distributed by Pathe. But in that same year, when the Pathe contract expired, Roach shifted distribution to MGM. As a result, for nearly a year, Roach comedies were being distributed by two companies simultaneously.

When the Laurel and Hardy partnership was formed in 1927, Stan was already 37 years old and Hardy was 35. Each had become a seasoned performer with some 20 years of solid experience on the stage and in films behind them. When the two joined forces, the result was hilarious.

Before teaming with Oliver Hardy, Stan Laurel (second row, right) was a member of the Roach Comedy All Stars lineup.

In the Laurel and Hardy comedies, the two comedians never used character names. They were unbothered by the fact that their own names were associated with two half-wit characters who were involved in antics of all kinds. Interestingly, the very private Hardy did not use his personal nickname, Babe, in any of the films. He was always called Oliver, or Ollie for short.

Laurel and Hardy (left) exchange glances in a scene from With Love and Hisses, *a 1927 film which co-starred James Finlayson (greeting women).*

When Laurel and Hardy first made their appearance in films together, the silent film era was coming to a close. On October 6, 1927, in New York, Warner Brothers premiered *The Jazz Singer*, the first feature film with synchronized dialogue and music. Reviewers and audiences were impressed. Laurel and Hardy, great pantomime artists that they were, decided that they could afford to use dialogue sparingly, and still be effective. They took advantage of the new medium, and critics marveled at how right their voices were for their characters.

Sound added a new dimension to their personalities. When they dropped a piano down a stairway, in *The Music Box,* their shrieks made the scene all the more funny. Listening to childlike Stan get tongue-tied when attempting to rattle off an idea drove the audience into hysterics.

The advent of the talkies changed filmmaking considerably. In silent films, scenes were photographed at the rate of 12 frames per second and projected at 24 frames per second; the action on the screen appeared twice as fast as it had been acted. In the talkies, sound and sight were recorded and projected at the same speed—24 frames per second. The action, therefore, had to take place at the speed at which it was to appear.

In addition, with the advent of talking pictures came a change in the structure of films. Scenes that had been necessary to explain plot development could now be eliminated. Spoken lines could accomplish the same objective—and more effectively.

Stan and Ollie made their first appearance as a team in Putting Pants on Phillip *in 1927.*

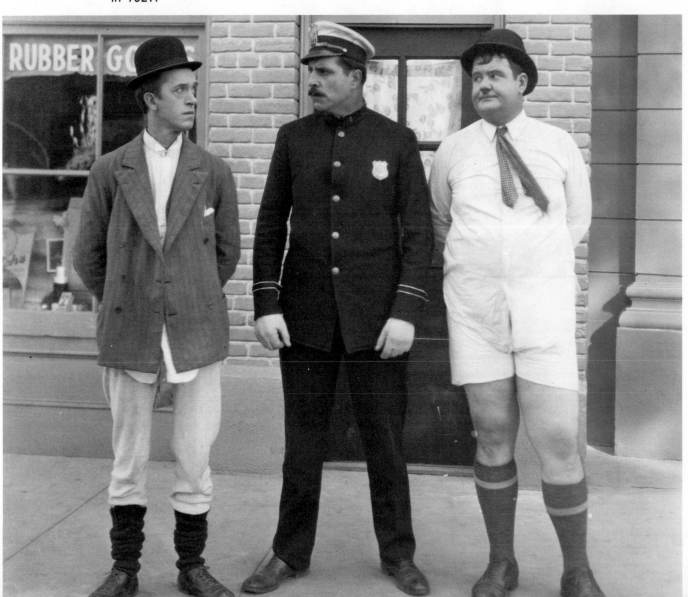

As talking pictures evolved, so did the characters of Stan and Ollie. Although their physical contrast made them easily identifiable, new elements were added to their characters. One writer of the era described them well: "Oliver is fine, round and juicy; Stan, little and dried up. Oliver is a grand, leisurely man with an elegant accent derived from the southern states. Stan is a fidgety, uncertain, timid little creature with an indefinable Lancashire-Cockney-Hollywood accent which only the English music hall could father."

Laurel and Hardy chose costumes which would be as appropriate to the personalities of their characters as possible. They wore stand-up collars and derbies to reflect a phony dignity. Babe combed his hair down over his forehead in a spit-curl bangs style. Stan made his eyes smaller by lining the inner lids. Very little general make-up was required.

Jimmy Finlayson (center) does an off-screen "routine" with a ketchup bottle for Laurel and Hardy in the Hal Roach Studios' commissary.

Hardy's way of standing, combined with his generous proportions and his under-sized derby hat, made him a funny sight even when doing nothing. Hardy was the "brains" part of the partnership. He delegated the dirty jobs to Stan, but the misfortunes inevitably fell on poor Ollie. Most of Ollie's troubles were due to his inablility to bend to circumstances; he would rather confront them head on.

Despite the fact that he was the cause of most of the misfortune, well-meaning but bumbling Stan always stood with a look of helpless amazement as he scanned the remains of a disastrous situation he had innocently caused. In short, his eagerness to be helpful was not a virtue.

Films of Laurel and Hardy always followed a recognizable theme. One critic described it well: "Hardy was the elephant on tippy-toe who always got stuck in the upper berths, daintily fingered his necktie, twitched his ridiculously tiny mustache, lost his too-small derby, and rushed with clumsy gallantry to the distress of fair damsels—only to trip over a broom that the simple-minded Laurel had left in the way."

Hardy's lips pursed in silly and childish exasperation was said to be an imitation of the stout, cross woman who once taught him in school. It was his best known expression. His windmill double take was a slight exaggeration of the favorite mannerism of a pompous and overweight politician he once knew. "Every time he was accused of negligence of duty," Hardy said, "he would reel and stagger as though he had been struck a mortal blow. He wound up in the pen."

Babe revealed to friends how he learned the distinctive style of a perfect southern gentleman. The favorite hand mannerisms, such as holding a tea cup with his pinky finger extended, was picked up during his youth when he spent time with his maternal Aunt Susie. He always referred to Susie as his favorite aunt and credited her with being the model for his good manners, courtesy and social grace. He had observed Aunt Susie entertain southern ladies and had studied their mannerisms. In being overly polite, in his acting parts, his intention was not to ridicule but rather to be utterly sincere . . . and for comedic effect.

Hardy's exaggerated dignity and self-importance, and his exasperated, mute appeals to the audience—made with a frustrated look directed towards the camera—endeared him to moviegoers. Behind the commanding worldly airs and courtly manners, such as tipping his hat graciously, Hardy also revealed an innocent child who could easily match the child in Stan. Hardy's character was designed to make him appear smarter, and, as he explained the character he was portraying, "There is no one as dumb as a dumb guy who thinks he's smart."

Stan played the role of the simpleton. Using a disarming smile and a childlike voice, he was happy to tag along and follow the instructions of Ollie. Stan's flat-footed walk, his armfold fall, his blank eye blink, his childlike cry and head scratch were movements and gestures that made him easily identifiable. Stan was the "child" of the team—and therein lies much of the secret of his success. Hal Roach explained it this way:

"Laughter comes from children; it's an emotion. . . . As far as people are concerned, the great comedians imitate children. . . . Hardy's action with the tie, Laurel scratching his head—these are the actions of a child. Laurel never cried when he was angry, he never cried when he was hurt, he never cried when he was scared. He only cried when he was confused—that's why it's so funny when he cries."

While the physical contrast of the two men did not, in itself, make them unforgettable, it did make them easily identifiable.

One of Stan's all-time favorite gags was to "inadvertently" spill gasoline on his thumb, then discover accidentally that gas would burn, and then convert his thumb into a cigarette lighter. With imbecilic smugness, he would hold the blazing thumb to Hardy's cigarette until the gas burned away and the flames reached the skin. He had gotten the idea, he said, when he saw a small town rake strike a match with his thumbnail, complacently hold it for a friend, and then double up in pain as the dislodged phosphorus began to smoulder under his nail.

One of Stan's favorite gags was spilling gasoline on his thumb and turning it into a cigarette lighter. Ollie looks on in amazement.

Laurel and Hardy's gestures were so expressive that little dialogue was needed. Some of the phrases they chose to use were repeated at timely intervals, such as Ollie's "Well, here's another fine mess," and Stan's "Hard boiled eggs and nuts."

Audiences knew what to expect as soon as the familiar faces of Stan and Ollie appeared on the screen: disaster! The same sight gags were used repeatedly, yet people laughed. Laurel's flip-flop walk, the vacant expression in his eyes, the head scratching, and the crying routine; and Hardy's stare of exasperation at the camera, his tie-twiddle and southern gentleman manners—all these never lost their humor.

The Laurel and Hardy comedy team meant many things to many people. Many years ago, a critic for the *London Times* wrote: "They represented to the world the frustrations and disappointments which daily confront the ordinary, frustrated individual. They were two men of peace, helpful and sympathetic— but they were also martyrs to incompetence. In each there was a strong streak of pathos. Laurel could look as dejected as a whipped mongrel. Hardy, so large, so magnanimous, so expansive, could have his self-esteem punctured as easily and as rapidly as a toy balloon."

Laurel and Hardy knew how to make the most out of puncturing dignity, which is the basis of slapstick comedy. Hardy had his theory: "A comedian has to knock dignity off the pedestal. He has to look small—even I do—by mental comparison. Lean or fat, short or tall, he has to be pitied to be laughed at. . . . The fun is in story situations which make an audience feel sorry for the comedian. A funny man has to make himself inferior."

Stan made this comment revealing his theory of comedy: "Keep a semblance of belief, however broad. Let your gags belong to the story; you must have a reason to motivate everything. . . . Let a fellow try to outsmart his audience and he misses. It's human nature to laugh at a bird who gets a bucket of paint smeared on his face—even though it makes him miserable."

The Laurel and Hardy comedies always had simple plots. Shooting scripts which directors ordinarily use were never prepared. All that was agreed upon in advance was a story outline, usually centered on one incident. A story outline could develop from the proposition of an enterprise, to the development of frustration in attempting its execution, and, finally, to misfortune and ruin that leaves the entrepreneurs in the same or a worse position than before undertaking the project. The project could be moving a piano, repairing an aerial, going on a picnic or painting a house. Laurel and Hardy were very talented at coming up with variations on the same theme. Stan was the major creative force; most of the gags were prepared by him.

Adept at improvising before the cameras, the comedy team would report to the set with only a basic idea in mind and an outline of what they planned to do. Because most of the creative work was done on the set, the timing of comics was often worked out by listening for reactions from the crew.

Most of the films that Laurel and Hardy made for Roach were shot in sequence, an expensive way of working and contrary to accepted film practice, but Laurel maintained that the end product would make the expense worthwhile. Everyone worked hard and, because labor unions did not yet exist, cast and crew kept working until they were satisfied with their product.

After the day's shooting, Stan remained at the studio to see the first rushes, do some editing, and then work up some gags for the next day's shooting. If Stan was dissatisfied with one day's takes, he would alter and improve the scenes, reshooting them when necessary. The final cutting version of the film was not made until the reactions of preview audiences could be studied.

Laurel and Hardy were experts at predicting audience reaction. They knew that an audience often laughed when they were able to anticipate what was going to happen. They knew, too, that although the same gags were used repeatedly, they could avoid monotony by providing their fans with the pleasure of *recognition,* another important factor in comedy. Familiar expressions, such as Stan's cry or Ollie's speechless appeals for help, became funnier and funnier as the years passed. Laurel and Hardy enthusiasts awaited and cherished these moments.

Visual comedy needs *time,* and the Laurel and Hardy Comedies allowed time for a gag to evolve and be reacted to. By avoiding too rapid a pace, they made sure that one laugh would not overlap another. They built their comedy leisurely and gracefully, extracting the most from every comic situation. In fact, Hardy sometimes required as much as 60 feet of film for a mere change of expression.

Laurel and Hardy never played for tears; nor did they play only for laughs. "Laurel and Hardy are interested in *human appeal* rather than in straight clowning antics," Hardy himself once said.

Although Stan and Ollie did not consciously attempt to avoid all social commentary in their work, it did creep into many of their more human comedies, of which they made many.

Mostly they played common people: waiters, peddlers, painters, carpenters, henpecked husbands, dog lovers, and salesmen. They also played sailors and French Foreign Legionnaires.

During their early years as a team at Roach Studios, Laurel and Hardy were given a free hand in developing the material they would use. They invented their own story lines and worked out their own gags. The atmosphere at the studio was friendly and relaxed; there were no strict rules and few schedules to be followed. And yet, the studio was determined to produce comedies of quality, placing emphasis on characterization and photographic excellence. By the end of the 1920s, Roach had surpassed Mack Sennett as the "king of comedy." In addition to his All Stars and Laurel and Hardy, he had the Our Gang Comedies.

The stock market crash of 1929 and the Great Depression years that followed didn't greatly affect the film industry. The public still needed entertainment and Laurel and Hardy were pleased to provide it. Stan explained the nature of their comedy to an interviewer in 1929: "People like to laugh at the misfortune of others. It's human nature. So we merely exaggerate those misfortunes. We multiply everything, making humor the very fact of repetition."

In an attempt to make people laugh, Laurel and Hardy films were very physical: cars were turned into accordions in head-on accidents and sliced in half by buzz saws; people would fall through picture frames, windows and roofs; houses were demolished. But the violence was never carried to the extreme, and the audience was assured that nobody was physically hurt. The violence merely served to puncture dignity, the secret of slapstick comedy.

Studio publicity photographers and press cameramen enjoyed taking pictures of Laurel and Hardy, who were always quick to strike a comic pose. The selection of publicity stills shown on this and succeeding pages were taken in the late 1920s and early 1930s.

The use of the physical to achieve humor is evident in the second film in the Laurel and Hardy Comedies series. *The Battle of the Century,* which stands to this day as a classic, featured pie throwing to end all pie throwing. A minimum of 2,000 pies were thrown in this picture (a figure that through the years has grown to 4,000 in some reports). The film was made in 1927, a time when moviegoers were becoming more sophisticated and were growing tired of the numerous pie throwing scenes in Mack Sennett's comedies and in Chaplin's *Behind the Screen.* It seems odd, then, that Laurel and Hardy would utilize the same device.

The idea of throwing so many pies in *The Battle of the Century* evolved during a gag session at the studio. A studio assistant suggested that one of the comedians throw a pie, but he was quickly hooted down. No better ideas were forthcoming. Then Stan got a brainstorm:

"Wait a minute! Suppose we do throw some pies, but let's throw more pies than anybody has ever thrown before. Let's throw so many pies that when we're finished nobody will ever throw another pie again!"

The plot for the picture was then decided: Laurel would be a prize fighter and Hardy his manager. A con man would convince Hardy that he'd never realize any funds from his fighting career and would advise him to take out an accident insurance policy on Laurel to make some quick money. Hardy would borrow money from Laurel to pay for the policy, and would then contrive a foolproof accident: Laurel would supposedly slip on a banana peel on the sidewalk. In his place, a delivery man (Charles Hall) with a tray of pies would slip on the banana peel and fall, and trigger off a laugh-getting epic battle royal—a sensational pie fight. Soon the whole neighborhood would be slinging pies at each other, while Laurel and Hardy stood on the sidelines keeping the busy participants in the melee supplied with pies.

For *The Battle of the Century,* the complete one-day output of the Los Angeles Pie Company was purchased—pies of all flavors. The movie displayed a staggering number of variations in the way pies can be thrown and their potential targets. Many call it the greatest Laurel and Hardy film ever made.

All Laurel and Hardy films were distinguished by their familiar theme music, "Coo Coo" (Ku Ku), written in a medium fast tempo by T. Marvin Hatley, then musical director for Hal Roach Studios. Hatley, who had begun his career with a three-piece ensemble in the early days of sound films, scored all of the Our Gang Comedies, all of the Charlie Chase films, and most of the Laurel and Hardy Comedies.

The "Coo Coo" theme had originally been composed by Hatley for a radio station for which he worked. "I got the idea from the common coo-coo bellows (murmuring sound, as of a dove)," he recalled about the Laurel and Hardy theme. "I combined a simple silly tune on top and the coo-coo below. The clash of the major second intervals is what makes it funny." One day Stan came up to the

"Well, here's another fine mess you've gotten me into, Stanley!"

The gestures and facial expressions used by Stan and Babe quickly became trademarks. So did often-used phrases, such as this one.

radio station, heard the tune, and expressed his desire to use it in his pictures. Hatley agreed and the theme was adopted.

All told, Stan and Ollie worked together in 14 films at Roach in 1927—all two-reel comedies. In 1928, their busy schedule continuing, the comedians made ten more two-reelers. What neither Laurel nor Hardy knew was that their star was just beginning to rise.

4.

Heyday Of Comedy

From their very earliest days as a team, Stan Laurel was given a free hand in the development of the Laurel and Hardy Comedies. The studio expected the team to turn out a two-reeler every two weeks, and Stan's expertise in developing story lines and editing film was a real asset. As Leo McCarey so aptly stated, "Stan had one of the best and most inventive comedy minds in history." As a result, the studio paid Laurel a salary twice that of his partner. Hardy was content to leave immediately for the golf course at the end of a day's filming while Stan stayed on, working.

Despite the attention Stan received for originating and building up gags for the films, and despite his higher salary, jealousy never existed between the two men. On the contrary, each had great admiration for the other's ability. Watching Babe Hardy on the screen in the studio's projection room, Stan sat at the edge of his seat, holding onto it tightly to keep from falling off as he broke into fits of laughter. Stan, who called himself the "Little Fellow," frequently laughed at his own gags, too. But when it came to judging comedy, Laurel was no "Little Fellow" at all.

Leave 'Em Laughing, a film made in 1928, did just that to its audiences. It featured two simple gags: a man in a dentist's chair alternately reacting to pain and laughing gas, and a traffic jam involving cop Edgar Kennedy. The film opens with Hardy trying to quiet the nerves of Laurel who is about to have his teeth extracted. Hardy sits in the dentist's chair to show Laurel how to relax, and, before he realizes it, the fast-working dentist gives *him* an anesthetic and extracts a tooth. Laughing gas is accidentally turned on and Laurel and Hardy both inhale too much of it. They laugh hysterically as they climb into their automobile and, when they find themselves in a traffic jam, continue their antics at a policeman's expense. By the time the traffic snarl reaches its peak, the cop is left minus his pants.

In all of their films, the comedians exhibited a great love for children, as is evident in this scene from Pack Up Your Troubles.

Although filmmaking was and is serious work, for Laurel and Hardy it was mostly fun. While shooting a scene—in which they were in bed together—for *Leave 'Em Laughing,* the comedians started giggling uncontrollably. They were unable to shoot that scene, or any other scene, that day. On the following day, the same thing occurred. On other occasions throughout the shooting period, the director was confronted with the problem of a crew that kept laughing uncontrollably and he was forced to yell "cut."

When Laurel and Hardy were at work, the lot, inevitably, became a center of attraction for all studio employees. "Let's go down and watch Stan and Babe. I feel like a good laugh," one studio employee would say to another. Having other actors or visitors on the set didn't bother the team. They had no time to become self-conscious; they were totally involved in their work. This is an interesting phenomenon when one considers that, personally, both Laurel and Hardy were quite self-conscious and, despite their fame, very modest. Both feared that people expected them to be as funny off-screen as they were on. Away from the camera, Babe was the kind of unassuming affable gentleman one would expect from a small boy raised in Georgia, and Stan was likewise a quiet, dignified home-loving man—the product of an English background. Neither ever used foul language or told an off-color story.

A 1928 film, *Two Tars,* one of the team's most famous, is an excellent example of their sense of humor. In *Two Tars,* Laurel and Hardy play sailors on leave. They rent a car and pick up two girls for a drive in the country. After a short time, they run into a heavy traffic tie-up caused by road repairs. All the delayed motorists are extremely irritated and suffering from very short tempers; they are in no mood to welcome Laurel and Hardy. A brawl breaks out and hoods, wheels and doors are yanked off. The virtually destroyed cars are finally driven away, some of them in pursuit of Laurel and Hardy, who lead them into a railroad tunnel just before a locomotive enters. The resulting confusion is hilarious.

In this scene from A Perfect Day, *a hilarious 1929 release, Laurel and Hardy go on a picnic with a bandaged Edgar Kennedy.*

Although the visual is basic to the comedy of the Laurel and Hardy Comedies, the importance of the extremely humorous dialogue is not to be overlooked. In one of their earliest talking films, *Men O' War,* made in 1929, there is a hilarious conversation between Hardy, portraying a sailor, and two beautiful, young girls. Finding a pair of women's panties on the ground (lost from a laundry basket), Hardy thinks they belong to one of the girls, but is too embarrassed to refer to the garment by name.

"Can you describe them?" he asks sheepishly.

"Well, they button on the side," she replies.

Hardy, embarrassed, pauses a moment to study the garment. He continues: "I'll bet you miss them."

"Well, you can just imagine," replies the girl. "They were so easy to slip off. Good thing we're having warm weather!"

Hardy laughs while the misunderstanding continues. Finally, a policeman finds the gloves and returns them to the lady.

Big Business, also made in 1929, was one of Laurel and Hardy's funniest visual comedies. Stan and Ollie played Christmas tree salesmen in California in mid-July; business was, of course, very slow. When they call at the home of James Finlayson to try to sell him a tree, they become involved in a battle over his refusal. Finlayson smashes Hardy's watch, and the war begins. By the time the battle has ended, Finlayson's home and some of its furnishings and landscaping are completely ruined, while Laurel and Hardy's car and their supply of Christmas trees are destroyed by Finlayson. The film ends with the parties forgiving each other, as Hardy presents Finlayson with a cigar that explodes.

Double Whoopee, made in 1929 by MGM, is a significant film in that it marked the first screen appearance of Jean Harlow, then 19 years old. It has been reported through the years that the beautiful platinum blonde got a small part in the two-reel comedy because it was less expensive for MGM to test her ability in this way than by holding a separate screen test.

The plot has Laurel and Hardy making an appearance at a plush New York hotel which is being readied for the arrival of a European prince. Laurel and Hardy are assumed to be the visiting royalty and are given very courteous treatment until their true identity—that of humble doormen—is discovered. In a scene with Harlow, her long dress is caught and partly torn off in the door of a taxi, and she arrives in the hotel unaware that her legs are showing.

The plot of *Brats,* a 1930 two-reeler, is simple, but interesting nevertheless. Laurel and Hardy play adults who baby-sit while their wives are away. Their children—through the use of trick photography—are played by *themselves.* Very large sets were built to emphasize the small size of the children. The story has the adults trying to play pool downstairs while the children become involved in horseplay upstairs.

Hog Wild, another 1930 production, also has a simple plot, but provided many laughs: an attempt to fix a wireless aerial on the roof of Laurel's house finds Hardy falling into a goldfish pond at least five times, but each time with a different gag, with the final fall created by showing a flight of birds and the sound of a tremendous splash.

The popular comedies of the 1930s often contained bathing scenes and the Laurel and Hardy films were no exception. (Left) Stan freezes in a bucket in Brats. (Below) The Fellows salute Jimmy Finlayson in Bonnie Scotland.

Laurel and Hardy's first feature-length film was *Pardon Us,* a six-reeler (55 minutes) made in 1931. The stars are imprisoned for brewing beer illegally during prohibition. Although the film was padded to stretch it to the required six reels, it contains many funny scenes.

Many of the gags in the Laurel and Hardy films were based on real-life experiences. The idea for the hilarious piano scenes in *The Music Box,* for example, originated when Stan and comedian Billy Gilbert were driving on Silver Lake Boulevard in Hollywood and noticed a building with a long, narrow flight of stairs. They immediately asked each other: "Wouldn't it be funny if The Fellows (they always referred to Stan and Babe's characters as "The Fellows") had to deliver something heavy up there?" A large, heavy piano requiring careful handling immediately came to mind. The idea was incorporated into a script. Other gags were added on location.

The Music Box, a three-reeler, brought Laurel and Hardy the Academy Award (the only one they ever received) for Best Short Subject of 1932. Laurel and Hardy artfully built their gag through repetition, evoking crescendos of laughter from audiences. Critics lauded *The Music Box* for its excellent "pacing."

Laurel and Hardy were enthusiastically greeted when they toured England in 1932.

Hal Roach produced several comedy series in the 1930s—the Our Gang films, the Charlie Chase films, and the Patsy Kelly-Thelma Todd films. But Laurel and Hardy proved to be the most popular with the public and, therefore, the most profitable to Roach. They had become established as expert pantomimists. But the team was not yet aware of its widespread popularity; few film critics, newspaper columnists or magazine reporters wrote much about them.

In 1932, when they decided to go on vacation together in England, Laurel and Hardy were amazed when mobbed by fans, reporters and photographers while changing trains in Chicago en route to New York. In New York, newsreel cars followed them down Broadway. In Southampton, a huge crowd awaited them at the docks. When they arrived in London, they were greeted by cheering fans, and in every city throughout England, Scotland and France admirers awaited them.

Stan and Babe relax atop a piano at a party in England in 1932. Douglas Fairbanks and Joan Crawford are seated second from right in this very rare photo from Lucille Hardy Price's private collection.

When they returned to the United States, Stan and Babe continued to make two- and three-reel films for Roach—until 1935. But, as short subjects were less and less in demand, and double-feature bookings a growing trend, Laurel and Hardy began to concentrate on making feature films.

Fra Diavolo (The Devil's Brother), a very humorous nine-reel (88 minutes) feature made in 1933, is a burlesque of a famous operetta. Critics had high praise for the film. One wrote: "Never have they put such enthusiasm into their work, and never have the gags flowed in such rapid and devastating fashion." A year later, they made another operetta, *Babes in Toyland,* and it, too, was enthusiastically received. Some critics label it the best of their operettas. Revivals seen in theaters or on television today are usually cut versions.

Away from the studio, Laurel and Hardy led lives that were distinctly separate. Hardy loved sports and activities of all kinds—golf, card playing, horses—and gourmet cooking. Laurel's major interests were boating and fishing.

Stan Laurel's 1926 marriage to Lois Neilson was happy in its early years. Lois gave up her acting career soon after they were married and concentrated on being a housewife in their beautiful, 14-room Beverly Hills home. On December 10, 1927, Lois gave birth to a daughter (also named Lois). Lois loved to cook for Stan and the child, but the couple entertained little because of Stan's long hours at the studio.

But, in May, 1933, Lois filed suit for divorce, stating that Stan said he did not love her, that he ignored her at parties, and that he had suggested that they separate. Within three months, they were reconciled. The reunion lasted two years. Then, on September 10, 1935, they were legally divorced. Stan, who never talked much of his love interests, commented that Lois and he continually got on each other's nerves to the point where "we could no longer laugh together."

Laurel did not remain single for long. Late in 1933, he met Virginia Ruth Rogers, a Los Angeles widow who worked for a clothing firm. They were married in 1934, but since his divorce from Lois was not yet final at the time, he remarried Virginia in 1935. Virginia, who Stan affectionately called "Baby Ruth," had been taught how to fish by her father when she was a little girl. She enjoyed going on fishing trips with Stan, and she was by his side on the day in 1935 when he proudly caught a 256-pound fish.

Stan and Virginia were happy together. "Stan was temperamental, but he was always sweet about it; if he did anything that hurt you, he'd always make up for it in a quick way," said Virginia. "He drank a lot, but he wasn't an alcoholic; he just drank for fun. He didn't drink at all when he was working."

Stan's daughter, Lois, visited him and his new wife quite often. Stan loved his daughter very much and Virginia developed a similar affection for her.

The Laurels lived in a comfortable home in the Chevoit Hills area of Los Angeles. Stan was financially secure, as the employment of three gardeners, a maid, a cook, and a combination butler/chauffeur would seem to attest to. In the

Stan holds his daughter, Lois, who appeared in several of the team's early thirties comedies.

living room, near a fireplace, was a big screen on which the Laurels would show films. They would usually invite four people for dinner and ask others to join them afterwards to watch the films. The Laurels spent happy days there, yet their marriage ended in divorce in 1937 when Stan told Virginia that he was involved with another woman. Stan's relationship with that woman turned out to be very brief.

In 1938 Stan married Vera Ivanoa Shuvalova, a Russian-born blues singer and dancer, known professionally as Illeana.

The marriage to Illeana attracted considerable national publicity. As the couple was settling into a Yuma, Arizona hotel, Virginia showed up shouting "bigamist." She protested that their divorce, which had become final the previous day, was *not* valid. She unsuccessfully tried to get the marriage to

Illeana annulled. To insure the legality of his marriage to Illeana, Stan remarried his Russian bride two months later in a Russian Orthodox Church.

It was during his marriage to Illeana that Stan was confronted by Mae, who had returned from Australia. Claiming to be Laurel's common law wife, she had filed suit in 1936 for monthly support, for lawyer's fees, for court costs, for a share of the comedian's property and for part of his annual earnings. A settlement was reached out of court for an undisclosed sum.

Meanwhile, in 1939, Lois filed suit seeking to have her alimony and child support raised substantially. The court denied her request.

In 1940, Illeana, known for sudden outbursts of temper, hit Stan on the head with a large frying pan and reportedly threw sand in his eyes during an argument. She sued for divorce, charging that he had threatened her with a gun and forced her to endure the company of his two previous wives. None of the statements were believed by the judge, and he directed the district attorney to prosecute her for perjury. Illeana immediately ceased making life difficult for Stan, and they were divorced in 1940.

Hal Roach Studios, which flourished in the 1920s and 1930s, later made films for the government.

Hardy, who owned a horse racing stable in the mid-thirties, towers over his jockey, Ralph Reeves.

Oliver Hardy had problems with his wife, Myrtle, and he, too, found himself in divorce court. Myrtle charged, in 1933, that he had lost $30,000 in one day, betting on horses at Agua Caliente, Mexico, and that he regularly dropped $100 to $175 a day on cards and golf. She also charged that he had been parading around town introducing another woman to acquaintances as Mrs. Hardy, and that he frequently stayed away from home all night. (Back in 1933, Babe had sued for divorce charging that she absented herself from home.)

The differences between Hardy and his wife were not resolved until 1936 when she appeared in court, asking $2,500 a month for separate maintenance, and charging that he was dating another woman. In turn, Babe charged habitual intemperance. On one occasion, he claimed she had left home in an intoxicated state with $35,000 in her possession. In 1937, a divorce settlement was finally reached: Myrtle was awarded $250 weekly, or 25% of Babe's earnings if they drop below $1,000 weekly.

Hardy's divorce was costly, but not as costly as his involvement with race horses. In the late 1930s, Hardy began to bet frequently. He bought his own stable of race horses, hiring a top trainer, a groom and a good jockey, Ralph Neeves. In 1937, Babe co-founded, along with Bing Crosby and others, the Del Mar Race Track in southern California.

Hardy invested a considerable amount of money in his racing venture, but usually he was too busy working or golfing to attend the races. When he once decided to watch his best horse, Manny, run in a claiming race at Santa Anita

Babe continued to bet on the horses even after giving up his racing stable in 1939. Here, he peruses a racing form.

(an event in which other owners may bid to buy the horses entered), he broke away from the studio early, but got tied up in a traffic jam and arrived too late to place a bet on Manny. The horse won, paid a good price, but somebody had claimed his horse. The incident led to his decision to quit horse racing as an owner, but not as a bettor.

Golf, an interest dating back to 1921 when he first played the game with Larry Semon at Los Angeles' Griffith Park, occupied much of Hardy's free time. He joined the Hollywood Country Club (now defunct), in 1926, and was one of the group of men who organized the Lakeside Golf Club near Hollywood, a club which was to become a prestigious club in the 1930s. Lakeside's members included famous stars of Hollywood's Golden Era: Bing Crosby, Randolph Scott, Guy Kibbee, Adolph Menjou, Don Ameche, W.C. Fields, Richard Arlen, Johnny (Tarzan) Weissmuller, Andy Clyde, Andy Devine, James Dunn, Frank Craven, Broderick Crawford, George Bancroft, Jack Oakie, Barton MacLane and many others, plus film directors, producers and screenwriters.

Very infrequently did Stan join Babe in a golf foursome. This was one of those occasions. With them are musician Jan Garber (third from left) and P.K. Wrigley.

Babe usually played in golfing foursomes with Kibbee, Menjou, Fields, Crosby, Ameche, and writers Grantland Rice, Henry McLemore and E. V. Durling. When not working at the studio, Babe would play 27-36 holes. When he was working, he would immediately head for the golf course after shooting his last scene hoping to get in at least nine holes.

"Babe never became an exceptional golfer, but he could hit a long ball and was a good putter," said Norm Blackburn, a screenwriter and television producer who played with him at Lakeside. "He gradually improved to where he got down to a 10-12 handicap."

(Left) In this rare photograph, taken in the early thirties, Hardy is decked out in his golfing attire. (Right) Actor Don Ameche was one of Hardy's golfing companions at Lakeside Golf Club. Here, Babe poses as his reluctant caddy.

Hardy created a lot of excitement at Lakeside when, in 1937, he moved into contention for the championship of one of the five classes, reaching the finals against Adolph Menjou after each of them had scored two upsets over favored contenders. At that time Hardy and Menjou were both about 18 or 20 handicap players. Bing Crosby told Blackburn about the match for an article in the club's fiftieth anniversary book:

"A lot of interest developed and a lot of tension, and they kept postponing the match. They were practicing in the meantime; I guess, trying to 'psych' each other. In the card room there was a lot of speculation and, finally, quite a book developed. They started laying the price. When they finally teed off there must have been $6,000 to $7,000 bet on the match. Menjou would give great speeches every day when he'd come into the card room. Babe was ducking him, Menjou would say. 'I'm at the peak of my game now and Babe knows it, and he's waiting for me to sluff off and then he's going to play.' But Babe didn't make any speeches; he just laughed, you know. They finally teed off and a hell of a gallery showed up from Hollywood. They had more people there than at the Los Angeles Open that year, I think. It was supposed to be 18 holes and it took them about seven or eight hours to play. They followed each other into the traps and into the rough and needled each other while they hit shots. I think Babe beat him on the last hole. It was a real sensational match. It drew many more people than the finals of the club title [the top flight]. Everybody had a bet going one way or another and I don't think either one of them broke 120."

John (Mysterious) Montague, famous golfer, visits Hardy at the studio commissary in this rare 1933 photograph.

One of Babe's best friends at Lakeside was John (Mysterious) Montague, a widely publicized golfer who had become famous not only for his prowess on the golf course but for his extraordinary feats of strength. They were steady companions, playing golf, cards, and dining together frequently. When Babe separated from his wife, Myrtle, after 12 years of marriage, and was awaiting the divorce, he didn't like living alone; he asked Montague to share his apartment in West Hollywood. About a month after the 1937 championship match with Menjou, Babe was surprised to find detectives arresting Montague at his apartment for allegedly having held up a road house seven years earlier in New York.

Montague, a former bootlegger who had gone "straight" during those seven years in Hollywood, was extradited as a fugitive from justice and brought to trial in New York. Hardy and others helped finance the lawyer's fees. Montague was eventually found innocent of the charges.

Hardy joined crooner Bing Crosby in a radio interview in 1937 marking the opening of Del Mar Race Track in California.

Much of Hardy's leisure time was also spent playing cards at Lakeside. Veteran announcer Harry von Zell regrets not having been able to capture the comedian's facial expressions on film during his games with Edgar Kennedy: "It was something to see; there was no dialogue between the two. . . . Hardy would take a long time to respond to Kennedy's bid while making the funniest expressions."

Babe, who had done much duck and quail hunting in the early thirties, went big game hunting in 1938 with Guy Kibbee in Utah. On the second day, he killed a deer and said he felt like the "worst criminal." The deer's eyes, he said, seemed to reproach him. This experience brought Hardy's hunting days to an end.

After his divorce from Myrtle, in 1937, Babe began dating other women. In July, 1939, while working on *The Flying Deuces* at Roach, Babe met a script clerk, Lucille Jones, in whom he became quite interested. She was a serious, hard-working woman who was helping to support her divorced mother, younger sister and brother. Lucille had worked for four years as a switchboard operator for Sol Lesser Enterprises at the old Pathe film studio. She later became a secretary to some writers in the script department. Lucille was beautiful, intelligent, had a pleasing personality; but she had no special interest in Hardy. At first, Lucille had disliked him because of the way he reacted when she reminded him that it was important to keep the continuity of a close-up scene identical to that of a master scene that had already been shot. Hardy assured her: "I *know* how it was, my dear; don't worry—I'll take care of everything." Although Babe remained very well-mannered and gentlemanly toward her throughout the picture, she continued to dislike him for no apparent reason.

Lucille remembered the fun she had working on Laurel and Hardy films:

"I was impressed with the fact they would improvise much of the comedy. In *The Flying Deuces, Saps at Sea,* and *A Chump at Oxford*—the pictures I worked

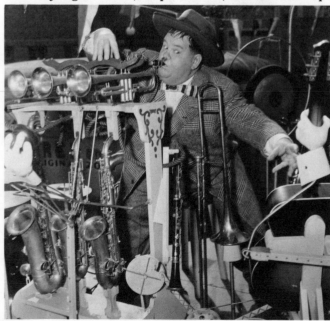

Hardy, who loved music, enjoyed gagging it up for this publicity shot for Saps at Sea in 1940.

Script Clerk Lucille Jones married Hardy in 1940.

on—they would go before the cameras without a script. I saw some of the story outlines, which would include typical Laurel and Hardy gag routines. They worked so beautifully together. They could feed each other lines—their minds clicked. They had great rapport with each other and could guess what the other was going to do next. I had never worked on comedies before and I was flabbergasted. I had so much fun on those pictures! I never knew what was going to happen. The cast and crew would often break up laughing. Stan and Babe were forever pulling gags on me.

"Babe proposed to me one morning at the studio after a story conference and gave me an engagement ring two days before Christmas. We had never gone out on a date together. However, he did frequently make it a point to come to the studio early when he knew I was doing typing work on scripts and get me a cup of coffee so he could talk to me.

"I'm sure it was Babe's eyes that finally won me over," said Lucille. "He had

Without their standup collars, derby hats and film make-up, Stan and Babe looked quite sophisticated.

the kindest, softest, most expressive eyes." She was also impressed by his thoughtfulness and concern for others. One day, she slipped on a rolled-up carpet at the studio. She fell backward, hit her head on a camera, and suffered a slight concussion. A huge box of red roses with a formal note wishing her a speedy recovery arrived; it had been sent by Babe. Soon, thereafter, Babe took Lucille out on their first date. It was New Year's Eve, and they went to dinner followed by dancing at the Roosevelt Hotel.

Babe and Lucille were married on March 7, 1940, in Las Vegas. "I didn't want a big wedding; always wanted it to be an elopement," said Lucille. "I took my mother, brother and sister along. We were married in the home of a judge by another judge. After the reception, we went to Riverside, California, and stayed in the bridal suite at the Mission Inn, arriving about midnight the same day. We then took a trip to El Centro, Indio, San Diego and Mexico."

When the Hardys returned from their honeymoon, they moved into a home they had already purchased on Magnolia Boulevard in the Sherman Oaks area of Los Angeles. It was a one-year-old house sitting on two and three-quarters acres. Bandleader Horace Heidt lived next to them, and cowboy star Buck Jones, who owned much of the vacant land surrounding the area, lived across the street. The Hardys settled down to a happy, married life.

Laurel and Hardy each had his own share of personal difficulties. But throughout the 1930s, they continued to produce superior films. Although their busy schedule had been reduced to four pictures in 1935, three in 1936, and two each in 1937 and 1938, it was the heyday of comedy and they continued to endear themselves to movie-goers everywhere.

5.

Years Of Decline

Although they had become firmly established as a team by 1928, Laurel and Hardy continued to sign separate contracts with Roach through the thirties. By hiring them as individuals, rather than as a team, Roach retained considerably more control and bargaining power. Each was well paid, but both Laurel and Hardy believed that, had they been contracted as a team, they would have earned higher salaries.

Periodic disputes arose over the fact that the comics were given individual contracts. In 1935, when Hardy's contract expired a year before Laurel's, Babe renewed his at an increased salary, but when Stan's contract came up for renewal, he refused the contract despite the fact that he was offered a higher salary. It was publicly announced that the team of Laurel and Hardy was breaking up because Stan Laurel refused to renew his contract. But within three weeks things were smoothed out and he signed a new four-year contract.

When Stan's contract expired four years later—in 1939—he was unhappy over the financial arrangements and decided not to sign another Roach contract. Roach refused to make any adjustment and Laurel did not work for an entire year.

With Hardy under contract alone, Roach decided to team him with Harry Langdon in a film called *Zenobia*, a comedy about southern life. The film was not a success: Hardy without Laurel was not as funny.

Roach, later in 1939, signed Laurel and Hardy to do two films *(A Chump at Oxford* and *Saps at Sea)*. This time they were hired as a team. In 1940, after the two pictures had been completed, the team formed Laurel and Hardy Feature Productions. Ironically, they did not produce films. Instead, early in 1941, Stan wrote a sketch in which he and Hardy entered a police station to get drivers'

Hardy wore spectacles for his role in Zenobia. He appeared in the 1939 comedy without Laurel, who had refused to renew his Roach contract.

licenses. Combining the sketch with variety acts and featuring many beautiful girls, they produced a 30-minute show called the *Laurel and Hardy Revue*. The revue toured legitimate theaters throughout the midwest and the east, performing seven days a week, four shows on weekdays and six or seven on Saturdays, Sundays or holidays. For three months they did a USO tour of the Caribbean. It was a strenuous schedule.

In 1941, Laurel and Hardy toured several major cities with a 30-minute live comedy revue.

Laurel and Hardy's popularity was reaffirmed in 1941 when they were wildly acclaimed at the Mexico City Motion Picture Festival where they made personal appearances in parades and other public events. Although they didn't perform, and no Laurel and Hardy films were shown, they drew more attention and applause than any of the other stars.

(Top) Joe E. Brown, one of Hollywood's greatest comedians, clowned with Stan and Babe in 1941 at the Mexico City Motion Picture Festival. (Bottom) Laurel and Hardy drew more applause than any of the other stars at the Mexico film festival. They were cited for Distinguished Service.

When they returned to the United States, Stan remarried Virginia Ruth Rogers. Soon thereafter, he was beset by legal problems, one of which stemmed from a claim by an English woman who charged that he had deserted her and their three children in England. Stan was able to prove to authorities that he was in the United States before her children were born.

In May, 1941, Laurel and Hardy signed an agreement with Twentieth Century-Fox, a considerably larger studio than Roach. At Fox, they soon discovered that they did not enjoy the freedom that they had at Roach. Whenever Stan suggested that new sets be built to enhance a gag, he was turned down. Fox was much more concerned with production schedules and profits than creativity. The team was seldom consulted on script content. Consequently, most of the routines in the six films they did for Fox between 1941 and 1945 were the usual Laurel and Hardy fare. Neither time nor money was available for the creation of fresh material.

The first film Laurel and Hardy made for Fox was *Great Guns*, in which they played the guards of a rich man's son. Fearing for the son who would have to be in the army by himself, they enlist and soon find themselves in trouble with a tough sergeant. The critical reaction to the movie was negative: the film was too slow moving, and contained very few good comedy sequences.

Great Guns, made in 1941, was one of six films the comedians made for Twentieth Century-Fox during World War II.

Great Guns was followed in 1942 by *A-Haunting We Will Go*. It was considered an improvement over the previous effort, but was criticized for being slowly paced and containing outdated material.

Laurel and Hardy's next Fox film was the 1943 *Air Raid Wardens*, in which they played air raid wardens who stop a Nazi plot to sabotage a magnesium factory. Those critical of the film said it had "too much repetition" and "childish appeal only."

They made two other films in 1943: *Jitterbugs*, in which Vivian Blaine played a night club singer whose career they were trying to help; and *The Dancing Masters*, which saw them as dancing school operators. *Jitterbugs* was rated as one of their better Fox films; *The Dancing Masters* was poorly received.

In 1944, Fox featured Laurel and Hardy in *The Big Noise*. As employees of a detective agency, they get involved with the inventor of a super-bomb. Reviewers panned it, calling it the worst of the team's full-length pictures.

The Bullfighters, a 1945 release, was the team's last Fox film. In it they again played private detectives—this time looking for a lady crook in Mexico. *The Bullfighter* was also poorly received. After the outbreak of World War II, Laurel and Hardy went on to make two films for MGM.

The eight films made by The Fellows in the four-year period between 1941 and 1945 (six for Fox; two for MGM) were not nearly as funny as the comedies they had made in the twenties and thirties. Stan and Ollie blamed this on poor material. Had they been provided with better gags and story lines, they maintained, they would have been much funnier. It was also true that Stan, who had passed his fiftieth birthday, was losing his innocent, childlike look. Hardy's screen image was not nearly so much affected; a mature, fat man could still be funny. Whatever the cause, Laurel and Hardy seemed to be losing their appeal. Moreover, Abbott and Costello films, which had caught on as popular wartime entertainment fare, were providing strong competition.

With the outbreak of World War II, Babe and Lucille joined the rest of the country in planting a Victory Garden. Babe, who had always been interested in food, enjoyed growing his own vegetables, and using them in his cooking.

"Babe was a gourmet cook and he taught me how to cook," said Lucille. "He didn't like to eat out; he preferred to cook up something special at home. Spaghetti and meat balls was one of his favorites. He'd spend the whole day making the sauce. He loved Italian food, but he loved food, period!"

Babe, 6-foot-1, usually weighed about 286 pounds. Once, when he started to diet, his weight went down enough to affect his movie character image, so he began to eat more than ever until his weight exceeded 300 pounds.

Throughout the 1940s, Babe enjoyed inviting his circle of friends over for dinner and card playing. "His friends had a regular once-a-week poker game and I never knew whether we'd have four or 20 people drop in, but Babe always helped with the cooking."

Announcer Harry Von Zell (center) and comedian Billy Gilbert joined Hardy in a dance act during a party at Eddie Cantor's home in the mid-1940s.

Jimmy Durante provides the music at the home of Eddie Cantor (far left). Joining Stan and Babe in song are (from left) announcer Harry Von Zell, Joe E. Brown, and comics Norris Goff, George Burns, Charles Correll and Cass Daley.

Babe continued his musical interests after he became a big film star. "He was always singing at home," recalled Lucille. "He played drums at the Lakeside Golf Club or on the set at the studio whenever he had the chance. He always wished he could've learned how to play the piano."

He also had opportunities to perform musically at the Laurel and Hardy Fun Factory, a theater especially built just behind his Sherman Oaks home in 1941. It comfortably sat 100 people. Lucille described it this way: "We had a regular stage with footlights where Babe and Stan rehearsed skits for their revues and tours; we also gave parties there. Hollywood stars, such as Red Skelton, performed there. We had a regular projection room with two machines and a full-size screen. We showed rented films."

The Hardys included among their friends Bob Hope, Don Ameche, Grant Withers, Loretta Young's first husband, Ed Callagan, husband of singer Ann Jamison of *Showboat* and the *Telephone Hour*, Bing Crosby, Bill Lawrence, producer of the Lux Radio Theater, and several non-show-business friends from the Lakeside Club.

Johnny (Tarzan) Weissmuller gets a physical from Stan and Babe in this 1940s photo.

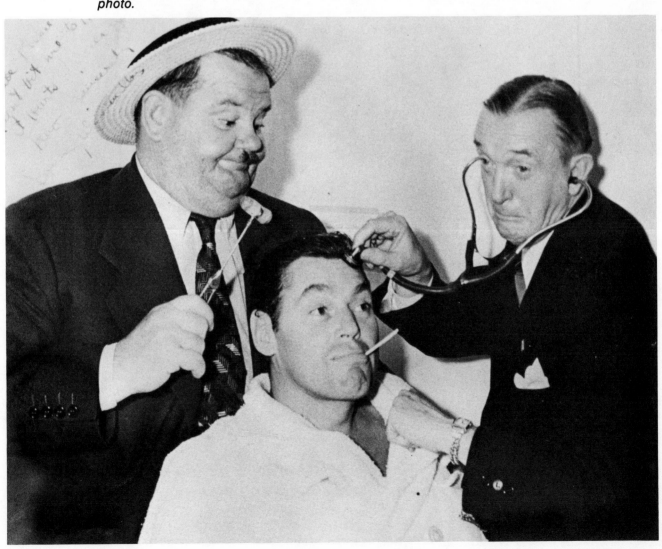

Although Hardy never socialized much with his teammate, Laurel, whenever they did, it was always amiable.

"They both respected each other's talents and there was no jealousy between them," said Lucille. "I believe one reason the team lasted so long was that they never saw each other much between pictures. They had their own group of friends and hobbies. Stan liked to surround himself with a lot of old-timers from vaudeville days. Stan always talked about films and stage arts; he lived it 24 hours a day. Babe had to get away from it."

Once during his World War II days at Fox, the time at which Babe was expected home from the studio had long passed, so he called Lucille. "Guess where I am? . . . I'm at the Beverly Wilshire. I stopped in here to have a drink and guess who I ran into?" He put Bing Crosby on the phone: "Lucille, we're here and we just can't get away. The bar's full of servicemen and they won't let us stop singing. Babe and I are both singing for them. I just didn't want you to worry. All right?" Lucille told them to keep singing.

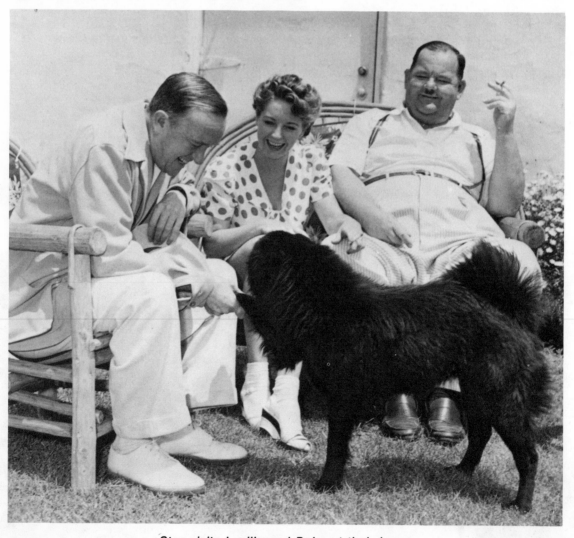

Stan visits Lucille and Babe at their home.

(Right) Lucille and Babe relax with their dog at their Sherman Oaks home in the 1940s. (Below) Hardy and comedienne Charlotte Greenwood had a good laugh during a party at the Hollywood Victory Caravan in 1943.

Stan and Babe were greeted by Hardy's wife, Lucille, in 1943 when they returned from a tour of entertaining servicemen.

Babe was known around Hollywood as a kindly gentleman, and there were times when people took advantage of his generosity. Anybody could approach Babe with a hard-luck story and he never turned them down. He was always ready to lend money. "Half the time he never got it back," reminisced Lucille. "Finally, after we were married several years, he started telling those who were seeking loans, 'I've got to talk to Lucille . . . she handles all the finances.' "

Hardy loved clothes and had all of his own custom-made. When questioned about his extreme fastidiousness, he emphasized that it's bad enough to see a fat man, but nothing worse than to see a *sloppy*, fat man.

Hardy had always been self-conscious about his weight, but justified it by explaining that fatness was necessary to his livelihood. Because of his size, he didn't like to attend previews; he was uncomfortable sitting in a theater seat. Lucille would go to the previews, and she and Stan would give reports on audience reaction. "In his early days, he'd go to previews so he could study himself and improve his mannerisms," said Lucille. "But when I knew him, he didn't like to see himself on the screen."

In 1946, Stan Laurel and Virginia Ruth divorced for the second time. Soon after the divorce, Stan married Ida Kitaeva Raphael, a Russian opera singer and actress who had been born in China of White Russian parents. Her previous husband, Raphael, was also distinguished in the concert world, and the two of them had traveled the concert stages together.

A candid shot of Stan, in the 1940s, when he was in court on divorce proceedings.

Stan Laurel and Oliver Hardy as they looked off-screen in 1947. Their last regular series of films was made during World War II.

Ida was tempermental and easily excitable, but fortunately this posed no problem, for she was an extremely devoted wife, and a very sincere person. She and Stan settled down on a Canoga Park ranch and got along splendidly. Unemployed entertainers were welcomed to their home, and Laurel did not hesitate to lend money to many, some of which was never returned.

Stan enjoyed his open-house policy as much as his visitors. He kept a well-stocked bar for the pleasure of his guests, most of whom were film and stage people. Despite these moments of joy, Stan remained unhappy about what had happened to his own film career.

In 1947, English agent Bernard Delfont signed Stan Laurel and Oliver Hardy for a stage tour of the British Isles. They were to be the first Hollywood personalities that Val Pernell, operator of the Palladium, imported to London. It had been two years since Laurel and Hardy finished their second and final picture for MGM, and they were thrilled about the opportunity.

Accompanied by Lucille and Ida, they embarked on the year-long tour which would take them to Denmark, Sweden, Belgium and France. Their schedule would be a busy one: performances every day of the week except Sunday. Sundays were reserved for traveling.

The three skits used by Stan and Ollie—a driver's license sketch, a hospital scene, and a railroad station act—were well received everywhere. But they were most successful in England, where the capacity audiences were best able to understand them.

Arriving in England for a stage tour in 1947, Hardy jokingly carries only the smallest luggage while Laurel is loaded down with heavy stuff.

Those who saw Laurel and Hardy in non-English speaking countries were astonished to learn that the comedians could only speak English. Admirers in Europe had heard them speak their own languages in films; they were unaware that back in the thirties Laurel and Hardy had "spoken" these foreign languages using scripts in which translators had phonetically spelled out each word. When audiences realized that their idols spoke only English, they were sorely disappointed.

Wherever Hardy went, he was immediately recognized. Laurel, reverting back to his English accent in England, did not have the same problem, for it was easier for him to become just another face in the crowd. There were many press receptions, meetings with Lord Mayors, and charity functions to attend. The

Laurel and Hardy received this congratulatory certificate when they performed before the King and Queen of England at the London Palladium in 1947.

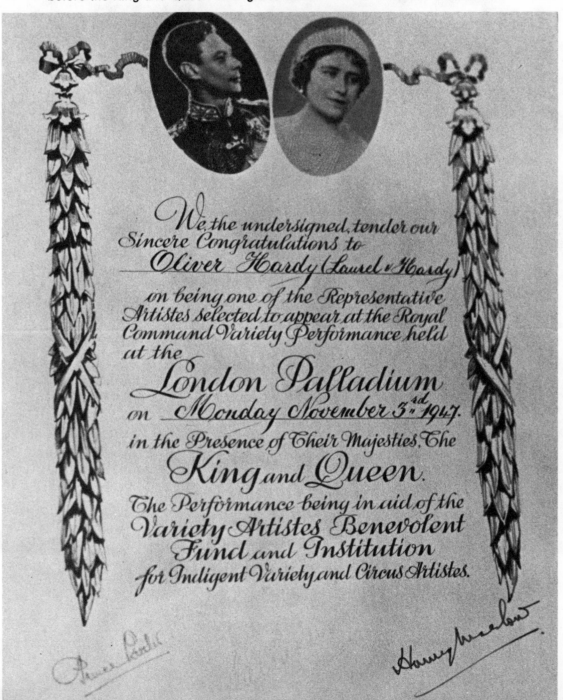

schedule was busy and exciting. By the end of the tour, Babe weighed under 200 pounds; the busy schedule, and food rationing, which was still in effect in the British Isles, were responsible for that.

At the conclusion of the tour, Stan and Ida boarded an ocean liner for the voyage home. The Hardys booked passage on a freighter carrying a total of 12 passengers. The 30-day trip was slow and relaxing. Lucille and Babe accomplished their mission: when they arrived home they were thoroughly rested.

Laurel and Hardy and their spouses visited the Standard Auto Works in Coventry, England, in 1947.

Laurel and Hardy did not make any pictures together for the next two years. Hardy did, however, appear without Laurel in *The Fighting Kentuckian*, a 1949 John Wayne western, and in Frank Capra's comedy, *Riding High*, in 1950.

In the spring of 1950, Laurel and Hardy traveled to France to make a film called *Atoll K*. The picture, produced by Raymond Eger for Les Films Sirius/Fortezza Films, was to be completed within 12 weeks. When they arrived in

Laurel, underweight from illness, in a scene with Hardy, heavier than ever, in Atoll K, *filmed in Paris in 1950-51.*

Paris, they found that adequate preparations for filming had not been made; not even a story had been written. Stan quickly wrote a story in collaboration with two writers from the United States.

An inexperienced director and crew led to more production delays. When Stan contracted a urinary disease, production was delayed still further. After recovery from an operation, Stan fell ill again, this time suffering from dysentery caused by bad food that he had eaten on the island location where they were filming. His weight dropped from 165 to 114 pounds. To compound matters, Laurel now also learned that he was diabetic. Medical facilities were provided for Stan on the set. With these facilities provided, he was able to work for a short period each day, until the picture was eventually completed—*one year* after he and Hardy had arrived in Paris.

Laurel and Hardy assigned much of the blame for *Atoll K's* poor cinematography on the French director, Leo Joannon, who, they said, must have thought he was shooting a travelogue. Joannon, wearing riding breeches and a pith helmet and equipped with several megaphones in varying sizes, spent three days shooting a lake because he thought it was a suitable photographic subject.

Atoll K was completed in the spring of 1951. Also released under the titles *Robinson Crusoeland* and *Utopia*, the film initially had no distribution in the United States. Three years after its release in Europe, a cut version was released in the United States, but critical reaction was poor.

Despite *Atoll K's* weakness, Laurel and Hardy remained popular in Europe between the years 1951 and 1953. *Our Relations*, an old film, ran more than six months in Germany, and *Fra Diavolo*, a 1933 film, was in its tenth revival in Italy.

It took Stan quite a while to recover from his illness after returning to California in 1951, but eventually he regained his strength and restored his lost weight.

Laurel and Hardy returned to England for a nine-month tour in September, 1952. They returned to England a year later, in September, 1953, again touring for nine months.

Hardy, backstage between shows, in England, cuts a cake celebrating his sixty-second birthday in 1954. Lucille is to his right; Stan and Ida are to his left.

*Hardy, wearing glasses, is sur-
rounded by a crowd of ad-
mirers in Grantham, England,
in 1952.*

Despite the fact that their film careers were over, and their best films were already 15 years old, The Fellows received a tremendous reception when their boat docked in Cobb, Ireland, during the 1953 English tour. Boats tooted their whistles and huge crowds awaited them, cheering madly. All at once, the church bells in Cobb began to ring out "Coo Coo," their movie theme song. The welcome so overwhelmed Laurel and Hardy that they were moved to tears.

In 1954, while still in England, Hardy came down with pneumonia and suffered a mild heart attack. When the 1953-1954 tour ended, the Laurels and the Hardys stayed in Europe for an additional week. They spent a pleasant week with friends and then boarded a freighter for the return trip to the United States.

Back home in 1954, Lucille Hardy was contacted by the producers of Ralph Edwards' *This is Your Life* television show. She was asked to work with Edwards' staff and the comedians' attorney and manager, Ben Shipman, on a proposed program about Laurel and Hardy. Edwards had decided to cover the lives of both men on the same program, the first time the show had ever attempted to do so.

"I tried to get Stan's sister here from England and Babe's sister from

Georgia, but neither of them could make the trip,"said Lucille. "We didn't inform Ida until a few days beforehand."

Lucille had difficulty making the necessary arrangements because Stan spent a great deal of time at home and enjoyed answering the telephone. This made it difficult to keep the secrecy that was required by the show's producers. "It took us a couple of months to get all the research done and people contacted."

(Top) The comedians enjoyed a 1953 visit to the Bull Inn, owned by Stan's sister and her husband, in Hungerford, Nottingham, England. (Bottom) Laurel and Hardy and wives pose aboard ship en route to Europe in the fall of 1953.

Babe, Lucille, Ida and Stan toast to the future aboard a Danish ship in 1954. Joining them is the ship's First Mate.

On the December night in 1954 when Laurel and Hardy were to be the subjects on *This is Your Life*, Stan, Babe and their wives were invited to the Knickerbocker Hotel in Hollywood to meet Bernard Delfont, their British agent, who had just arrived in the United States. When television cameras entered Delfont's hotel room to witness the reunion, Stan and Babe were stunned. "They were thoroughly flabbergasted," recalled Lucille. "Walking from the hotel to the television studio, they both kept repeating, 'I can't believe it . . . I never thought anything like this would happen to me.' They were shocked and overwhelmed by it."

Stan, a perfectionist who didn't like to make a public appearance without a detailed rehearsal, said only a few words during the entire program. Hardy was not as concerned about not being prepared, but his answers to all questions were also brief.

Laurel and Hardy each received a gift of a 16mm sound film of the program and a Bell & Howell sound projector. Several months later, after again viewing the film of *This Is Your Life*, Stan became very unhappy about it. "We never should've done it," he told his friends. "Why do they do things like that? They should've had a script."

One of the things that tormented both Stan and Babe in their declining years was that many of their old films were now being shown on television and they were receiving no income from these reruns because no provision had been made for it in their contracts. Appearing on live television seemed to be the only hope of continuing their careers as a comedy team. They feared that any television appearances they made would be affected by competition from their own rerun films. These fears, however, were for naught. While the reruns helped boost their popularity, they did not receive any offers to appear personally on television. Finally, in 1955, Hal Roach, Jr. proposed a series of filmed television specials. They never materialized, mostly because of health problems that beset the comedians.

(Left) Stan and Babe pose with a studio publicity man during the dedication of Lake Laurel and Hardy at Hal Roach Studios in 1954. (Below) Laurel and Hardy pose with actor Charles Farrell and actress Gale Storm (My Little Margie) at Hal Roach Studios in 1954.

In April of 1955, Stan suffered a stroke which left him with stiffness in his left side. Hardy's health had begun to fail more and more in 1955. He suffered gall bladder attacks, heart attacks and a kidney infection. "He didn't want to let people know he was sick . . ." Lucille revealed. "He didn't go anywhere. Then, on September 12, 1956, he had a massive paralytic stroke and suffered brain damage. [He was treated at St. Joseph's Hospital, Burbank.] Specialists were called in, who said that he might last two days or two weeks. After his stroke, he couldn't talk, he couldn't write, he couldn't move. All he could do was read and watch television, and that, too, became difficult for him to absorb and comprehend."

Hardy with a group of Hollywood stars in 1955. Seated are John Wayne and Jack Carson. Standing are Grant Withers, Dennis Morgan, Forrest Tucker and Wayne Morris.

After his stroke, Babe's only method of communication was a feeble motion that he was able to make with the fingers of one hand. Stan came to visit him once on one of Babe's better days and he recognized Stan. Unable to speak to him, he carried on a conversation with gestures.

Lucille was constantly at Ollie's side during his stay in the hospital. He had been bedridden since September, 1956, when he suffered the stroke. When he was released from the hospital in February, 1957, the Hardys moved into the home of Lucille's mother in North Hollywood. Babe lay in a room cluttered with hospital equipment and was cared for by nurses around the clock. His once over-sized body wasted away to a mere 145 pounds.

Oliver Norvell Hardy, after suffering two more strokes, went into a coma. He died two days later, on August 7, 1957, 11 months after his first stroke—at the age of 65.

Masonic funeral rites for Hardy were held at Pierce Brothers Mortuary in Beverly Hills. Following cremation, his remains were interred at the Garden of Hope, Valhalla Memorial Park, North Hollywood.

Stan, who was in poor health, was advised by his doctors not to attend the funeral. He expressed his grief with these words: "He was like a brother to me. This is the end of the history of Laurel and Hardy."

For Lucille, who had been married to Babe for 17 years, the loss of her husband was tragic. "When Babe died, I just died with him," she lamented. "It was the end of the world as far as I was concerned."

Bandleader Horace Heidt, standing to the left of Hardy's widow, Lucille, announces his intention of building an apartment complex on the site of Laurel and Hardy's Fun Factory in 1961. Actress June Darwell is seated. Beatrice Kay is third from right. Chet Conklin is at far right. Standing, center, is Francis X. Bushman.

After her husband's death, Lucille stayed for a time with her sister and brother-in-law in Palm Springs. She enrolled in a real estate school, passed her state examination, and returned to live in the San Fernando Valley, where she rented an apartment in North Hollywood. In 1960, she married Ben Price, a former featherweight fighter from Cleveland. Price had founded the *Valley Times* newspaper in Los Angeles in 1939, and later worked for the *Hollywood Citizen News*. After that he entered the insurance business. As of 1976, Lucille and Ben Price still live in a comfortable apartment in North Hollywood. She continues to answer mail inquiries about Oliver Hardy.

Lucille Hardy Price, widow of Oliver Hardy, keeps up correspondence with the comedian's fans. This photo was taken in 1975.

From the time he suffered a stroke, Stan had spent most of his time indoors. He had moved out of his Canoga Park ranch in 1948. At the time of Hardy's death, Stan and Ida lived in the Oceana Hotel, on Ocean Avenue in Santa Monica, overlooking the Pacific. Sightseer bus tour operators let passengers know that Stan lived there, which resulted in many eager fans knocking on his door. The unpretentious comedian talked to many of them. Movie and television stars, particularly comedians, also sought him out.

Stan's telephone number was listed in the directory. He received telephone calls from all over the country, at all hours of the day and night. When a book about Laurel and Hardy was published in 1961, his fan mail increased considerably. He tried to answer as much of it as he possibly could.

In 1961, Stan Laurel was awarded a special Oscar by the Academy of Motion Picture Arts and Sciences for his contribution to film comedy. He was a very proud man!

Reports circulated in 1964 that Laurel was in bad financial straits. The rumors were attributed to a British newspaperman who had written an article to that effect. In truth, although he wasn't wealthy, Stan lived comfortably off insurance annuities in his retirement days. He told friends that he was as rich as a millionaire because he had Ida, a mate who throughout the years had always remained devoted to him.

Actor Dana Andrews presents Laurel with a special Screen Actors Guild award in 1963. During his school days, Andrews used to run Laurel and Hardy two-reelers at a local theatre.

Stan passed the early 1960s watching television, including his old films. Although he enjoyed them, he was perturbed by the way Laurel and Hardy films were cut to accommodate advertising messages.

On February 23, 1965, 74-year-old Stan Laurel suffered a heart attack and died. His funeral was held at the Church of the Hills in Hollywood Hills, where Dick Van Dyke delivered the eulogy. After cremation, he was buried in the Court of Liberty in the new Hollywood Hills Forest Lawn Cemetery. A plaque above his grave reads:

STAN LAUREL
A Master of Comedy
His genius in the art of
humor brought gladness
to the world he loved.

Marcel Marceau, the master mime who had been helped by Stan and Babe in getting his start on the stage, said of Laurel:

"Stan Laurel was one of the great mimes of our times, expressing the struggle of man between light and shadow, laughter and tears. He belonged to those incomparable artists who made a Golden Age of the American silent films. Without them the movies would not have grown as they did. Stan was not only a true artist, but was also a true human being. I'm proud to say he was also my friend."

6.

A Growing Cult

The memory of Laurel and Hardy lives on in the hearts of millions. A cult that began in the late 1950s continues to flourish in the mid-1970s.

In the late 1950s, and through the middle 1960s, several compilations of footage from Laurel and Hardy's greatest features and shorts were made. Robert Youngson Productions released the *Golden Age of Comedy* in 1958, which featured Laurel and Hardy along with many other comedy stars of the 1920s and early 1930s. The feature not only gave audiences an opportunity to laugh at many of the old comedians once again, but served as an important vehicle that stimulated renewed interest in Stan and Ollie. Youngson followed *The Golden Age of Comedy* with *When Comedy Was King, Days of Thrills and Laughter, Thirty Years of Fun, MGM's Big Parade of Laughs, Laurel & Hardy's Laughing Twenties*, and *The Further Perils of Laurel & Hardy*. Jay Ward Productions produced *The Crazy World of Laurel & Hardy* in 1966. The ads for *Laurel & Hardy's Laughing Twenties* included a sworn survey by George Fine Surveys, Inc. which claimed that it clocked 253 laughs—"A record for laugh content of any comedy we have measured in our 30 years of experience."

In the middle and late 1960s many loyal Laurel and Hardy fans proved that they were eager to do more than merely look at the films of their favorite comedians. It happened in this way: several months before the death of Stan Laurel, John McCabe, who had become a friend of Stan's while authoring a book entitled *Mr. Laurel and Mr. Hardy*, helped to found an organization called Sons of the Desert. Similar to the Sherlock Holmes group and the Baker Street Irregulars, the organization, deriving its name from a 1934 Laurel and Hardy film in which the comedians pledged their loyalties to a national lodge called Sons of the Desert, was devoted to Stan Laurel and Oliver Hardy.

"Stan was delighted with the idea and, when I drew up a constitution for the organization, he approved," said McCabe.

Article I of the Sons of the Desert constitution describes its purpose: ". . . an organization with scholarly overtones and heavily social undertones devoted to the loving study of the persons and films of Stan Laurel and Oliver Hardy."

Robert Youngson advertised The Further Perils of Laurel and Hardy, *which contained excerpts from many of their films, as "a fountainhead of fun!"*

The original Sons of the Desert organization was founded in New York in 1964 by a group of Manhattan literary and show business people which included Orson Bean, Al Kilgore, John McCabe, Chuck McCann and John Municino. Sons of the Desert now has chapters (or "tents" as their members refer to them) in 25 major cities across the country. Nation-wide membership is estimated at 1,000 persons. The New York club is the largest tent with approximately 300 members, and is followed by Minneapolis with 175, and Philadelphia with 125.

Each tent is named after a Laurel and Hardy film: Two Tars, Block Heads, Way Out West, Tit for Tat, Brats, the Flying Deuces, and the Dancing Cuckoos are some. One of the newest tents was organized in 1975 in Calgary, Alberta, Canada.

Tent meetings are open to anyone who loves and respects Laurel and Hardy and their work—with one restriction: members must be 18 years of age or older. Meetings are held no less than four and no more than 12 times per year. The groups meet, have dinner, enjoy the showing of Laurel and Hardy films, and spend a social hour during which refreshments are served.

Members claim that Sons of the Desert is not a typical fan club. They prefer to call themselves "buffs."

"We are emphatically, almost aggressively, *not* a fan club," said McCabe. "A 'fan' is someone who is totally uncritical, and a 'buff' is somebody who is more discriminating. He loves the objects as much as a fan; he also realizes that the thing he loves isn't necessarily the greatest to hit this planet." In addition to the charter members, mentioned above, the membership of Sons includes notable entertainment figures Dick Van Dyke, Soupy Sales, Dick Cavett, Dick Martin, Jonathan Winters and Sammy Davis, Jr. The age range of the membership covers fans who saw the Laurel and Hardy films when they were first released, to younger members who have only recently become acquainted with the comedians through television. While Sons of the Desert was initially a stag group, the tents now (with the exception of the New York chapter) welcome both sexes. The Block Heads tent in Minneapolis-St. Paul has about 75 female members.

When McCabe appeared on NBC's *Today* show, he received more than 1,000 letters requesting information on how to join.

The Way Out West tent, located in Van Nuys, near Hollywood, has had many distinguished guests at its meetings. Lucille Hardy Price, widow of Oliver Hardy, and Virginia Ruth Laurel, Stan's former wife, have both attended. Others who have attended meetings are Ida Laurel, Hal Roach, Babe London (she played the fat lady in *Our Wife*), the late Billy Gilbert, and Lois Brooks, Stan's daughter.

Another Fine Mess, the Detroit tent, awards a trophy every year to the man, or men, who have "contributed *a fine mess* to Detroit." The city's weathermen were winners one year. This tent has the good fortune of having access to the 35 Laurel and Hardy films owned by Eric Stroh of the Stroh Beer dynasty.

In Minneapolis, tent members wear derbies to meetings. Members of most tents wear Shriners-style hats (fezzes) as seen in *The Sons of the Desert* film.

Lois Brooks, in dress, attended the Sons of the Desert Way Out West tent's June, 1975 meeting. A birthday cake was served in honor of her father, Stan Laurel.

Lucille Hardy Price and her husband, Ben, attended the New York Sons of the Desert's tenth anniversary banquet.

Nearly 1,000 persons attended the New York tent's tenth anniversary banquet held in the ballroom of the Roosevelt Hotel in 1974. Lucille Hardy Price and her husband, Ben, were among the honored guests. *Babes in Toyland*, a 1934 Laurel and Hardy film, was screened.

The San Diego tent has a scholarship fund to send students to UCLA. Other tents contribute to the fund too.

One of the most dedicated tents is located at the Connecticut Correctional Institution in Somers, Connecticut. Many of the inmates belong to the group, which is named after the first Laurel and Hardy feature film, *Pardon Us*.

The Flying Deuces tent of northern New Jersey was founded in 1968 by a group of discharged M.A.S.H. (Mobile Army Surgical Hospital) personnel sharing a common bond—the love of Laurel and Hardy. A Laurel and Hardy film night held in 1975 attracted 250 young children who jumped wildly at the sight of Stan and Ollie. The club provided the children with paper fezzes, making it look like a junior Shriners' convention. The evening was a huge success.

Dr. Jerry L. Greenburg, wearing a Laurel and Hardy tie, took autographs from the relatives and friends of Laurel and Hardy at Sons of the Desert meetings. He rises at 5:00 a.m. each morning to watch Stan and Ollie on television. A nice way to start the day!

THE INTRA-TENT JOURNAL

VOL. 2 No. 3   MARCH, 1975

Lucille and Ben Greet N.Y. SONS

Autumn came late to the Mother Tent of the SONS OF THE DESERT. After the traditional summer session (with no business· conducted) in August, the SONS were prepared to begin the fall, as usual, with a regular September get-together. Only, there was no such meeting. Because of difficulties concerned with the future stability of The Lambs, the hallowed Club where the SONS are headquartered, it was impossible to schedule a date for the September meeting, and October was nearly as much of a problem. As a result, for the first time in several years, the Mother Tent had to go elsewhere. The Hallowe'en program in October took place at the nearby Hotel Edison, where the Mother Tent used to gather prior to settling in its permanent home at The Lambs. But in November, the Lambs' affairs were in brighter condition. The financial outlook of The Lambs is now reported extremely poor, and it is expected that the SONS will need to relocate in the future.

The Mother Tent was back in high gear at The Lambs for the Christmas party, which, next to the annual banquet in June, is the SONS' biggest function of the year. The 1974 party, it is generally conceded was one of the happiest conclaves in a decade of such Yuletide celebrations. In addition to a screening of the feature, BABES IN TOYLAND, a Betty Boop cartoon and a Three Stooges comedy, there was live entertainment by singer *Phyllis Craig*, comic *Howard Itzkawitz*, comic *Adam Keefe*, and inimitable singer-improvisationist *Steve De Pass*, and his accompanist, *Gene Steed*. The latter act was so well received that the pair were accorded *two* standing ovations. (*De Pass*, who the Mother Tent has been trying to line up for a Holiday party for a few years now, is always extremely busy; he and his gifted accompanist just returned from a national tour with *Liberace*).

Continued on Page 4

The New York Christmas Gala! (Left) Steve De Pass, and accompanist Gene Steed steal the evening; (Upper Right) President Tye Morrow is questioned by Santa Claus (Frank Melfo); (Lower Right) Comedian Adam Keefe.

A CLEAR PICTURE OF STAN LAUREL

It is fitting that John McCabe has dedicated his book on Stan Laurel to both Ida (Stan's widow) and all SONS OF THE DESERT everywhere. Unlike the earlier work on the boys which was concerned with the chronology of their lives and films, this book is less constrained and concentrates on the human qualities and comedic genius that so typified Stan Laurel.

The book, which is rapidly paced, begins with Stan's life in early Music Hall days and builds to his final seaside retirement. Excellent insight is given into Stan's rationale for comedy that isn't always evident in his films. Unlike any other book concerning Stan, we are given a good view of his personal life which undoubtedly had much effect upon his work. At times, Stan is so vividly described, it feels like we could reach out and touch him. Also, Stan's relationship with Babe Hardy is aptly pictured through all those years on and off the screen. There are some interesting insights into Babe Hardy's off screen personality interspersed throughout.

A number of the scripts, performed for live audiences in later years are reproduced in their entirety. As familiar as we are with the voices and mannerisms of the boys, it's easy to visualize them in action.

The last part of the book perhaps, is best described as poignant. Stan's final days were so different from his earlier productive ones. But evidently his love of comedy which he related to most of life's simple situations never left him. He was truly a genius and few have been his equal.

R. L. G.

Roger L. Gordon, a college professor, edits The Intra-Tent Jounal *for the Sons of the Desert.*

Most tents publish newsletters to keep their members informed about activities. Roger L. Gordon of Huntington Valley, Pennsylvania edits the *Intra-Tent Journal* which contains news about other tent events.

John McCabe has suggested that those interested in forming a tent in their area or wishing to know the location of the tent nearest them should write to him at Box 363, Mackinac Island, Michigan 49757.

The constitution of the Sons of the Desert reads as follows:

CONSTITUTION

SECTION ONE

Article 1.   The Sons of the Desert is an organization with scholarly overtones and heavily social undertones devoted to the loving study of the persons and films of Stan Laurel and Oliver Hardy.

Article 2.   The founding members are Orson Bean, Al Kilgore, John McCabe, Chuck McCann, and John Municino.

Article 3.   The Sons of the Desert shall have the following officers and board members, who will be elected at an annual meeting:
a.   Grand Sheik
b.   Vice-Sheik (Sheik in charge of vice)
c.   Grand Vizier (Corresponding Secretary)
d.   Sub-Vice-Vizier (Treasurer and in charge of sub-vice)
e.   Board members-at-large (this number should not exceed 812)

Article 4.   All officers and members of the board shall sit at an exalted place at the annual banquet table.

Article 5.   The officers and members of the board shall have absolutely no authority whatever.

Article 6.   Despite his absolute lack of authority, the Grand Sheik or his deputy shall act as chairman at all meetings, and will follow the standard parliamentary procedure in conducting same. At the meetings, it is hoped that the innate dignity, sensitivity, and good taste of the members assembled will permit activities to be conducted with a lively sense of deportment and good order.

Article 7.   Article 6 is ridiculous.

Article 8.   The Annual Meeting shall be conducted in the following sequence:
a.   Cocktails
b.   Business meeting and cocktails
c.   Dinner (with cocktails)
d.   After-dinner speeches and cocktails
e.   Cocktails
f.   Coffee and cocktails
g.   Showing of Laurel and Hardy films
h.   After-film critique and cocktails
i.   After-after-film critique and cocktails
j.   Stan has suggested this period. In his words: "All members are requested to park their camels and hire a taxi; then return for 'One for the desert!' "

Article 9. Section "d" above shall consist in part of the following toasts:
1. "To Stan"
2. "To Babe"
3. "To Fin"
4. "To Mae Busch—who is eternally ever-popular"

Article 10. Section "h" above shall include the reading of scholarly papers on Laurel and Hardy. Any members going over an 8½ minute time limit will have his cocktails limited to fourteen in number.

Article 11. Hopefully, and seriously, The Sons of the Desert, in the strong desire to perpetuate the spirit and genius of Laurel and Hardy will conduct activities ultimately and always devoted to the preservation of their films and the encouragement of their showing everywhere.

Article 12. There shall be member societies in other cities called "Tents," each of which shall derive its name from one of the films (Two member tents have already been formed: The Another Fine Mess Tent of Canada [Vancouver, B.C.] and the Dancing Cuckoos of Detroit).

Article 13. Stan has suggested that members might wear a fez or blazer patch with an appropriate motto. He says, "I hope that the motto can be blue and gray, showing two derbies with these words superimposed: 'Two minds without a single thought.' "

SECTION TWO

To maintain a certain dignity at all costs, at all times the Way Out West Tent also subscribes to the following specific articles:

Article 1. Meeting place should be permanent (except for the annual dinner) and should be held in the vicinity of North Hollywood, Studio City, Hollywood or Tuluca Lake near Burbank. They should be held a minimum of 4, and a maximum of 12 per year, to be determined by the Executive Committee.

Article 2. Annual Meeting:
a. Between September 15 and November 15
b. Purpose:
1. Gala event (climax of year—special program—special guests)
2. Recognition of past service
3. Recognition of present service
4. Recognition of special people
5. Election of new officers

Article 3. In addition to the officers mentioned in Article 3 of Section 1, the following are the officers for the Way Out West Tent:

Executive Committee (all members of the Executive Committee shall forfeit their position if absent for two meetings for reasons unacceptable to the Executive Committee. (Members to serve 2 years, then Sheiks move up.)
a. Grand Sheik
b. First Vice-Sheik (program)
c. Second Vice-Sheik (membership and initiation)

    d. Third Vice-Sheik (fund raising)
    e. Grand Vizier (secretary and corresponding secretary)
    f. Sub-Vice-Vizier (treasurer)
    g. Second Sub-Vice-Vizier (Pratfall representative publicity) (non-elected position)
    h. Past Grand Sheik (nominations)

Article 4.   Membership—(fee is due by June 1st of each year) (includes—membership card—copy of constitution certificate membership) Members must be 18 years or older. Anyone under 18 must be approved by the Executive Committee.
    a. *Sponsoring:* contribution of $50 or more a year—Provides 4 guest passes—special sponsoring certificate (includes Pratfall) name will be listed on letterhead unless otherwise requested.
    b. *Active:* $20 a year or $35 a couple same address plus 2 guest passes. (Pratfall one issue per couple at same mailing address).
    c. *Student:* $5 per year and 30 hours or more of participation on committee assignments.
    d. *Honorary:* Relatives or families of our heroes and special celebrities (determined by the Executive Committee).

Article 5.   *Guest Passes:* are for one person for one meeting free. This does not include Honorary memberships which are at the discretion of the Executive Committee. Passes are not allowed to be used at initiation meetings. The guest passes are valid for the year of membership only.
    a. Additional guest passes may be purchased for $2.
    b. A guest may attend no more than 2 meetings on guest passes.
    c. New members joining for the first time shall participate in an appropriate initiation ceremony determined by the Executive Committee.

Article 6.   *Committee:*
    a. Program and decorations (under direction of First Vice-Sheik)
    b. Membership (under direction of Second Vice-Sheik)
    c. Fund raising (under direction of Third Vice-Sheik)
    d. Pratfall (under direction of Second Sub-Vice-Vizier)
    e. Awards (under direction of Executive Committee)
    f. Nominations (under direction of Past Grand Sheik)

Article 7.   No member shall use the Way Out West Tent of Sons or Sons of the Desert for personal gain, and shall in no way damage or degrade the reputation of the tent.

Article 8.   A membership may be revoked by 2/3 vote of the Executive Committee.

Article 9.   *Pratfall:* Pratfall is the official publication of the Way Out West Tent and not of any individual and is under the complete jurisdiction of the Executive Committee of the Way Out West Tent.

In 1970 a wave of nostalgia swept the United States. Interest in movie stars of the past: W.C. Fields, Humphrey Bogart, James Dean, Clark Gable, Stan Laurel and Oliver Hardy soared. The fascination with Laurel and Hardy, in particular, was explained by one enthusiast: "They provide a harmless laugh for everyone. No complications in scandals, and no politics." Laurel and Hardy represent an era of comedy that may be gone forever; their free-form zaniness is free of social message. The public longs to return to the simple, less problem-ridden past.

The official logo of the Sons of the Desert is used on the stationery of all affiliated clubs.

Books on Laurel and Hardy and showings of their old films on television and at theater festivals have contributed much to the growing interest. Whereas stations like WCCO-TV in Minneapolis-St. Paul began showing Laurel and Hardy films in the mid-1950s, in the fall of 1969 these comedies began drawing more substantial audiences when they were aired on a children's show from 10 to 11 a.m. on Sunday mornings. The A.C. Nielsen Co. reported that 316,000 watched Laurel and Hardy on an average Sunday morning: 137,000 viewers were 18 years old or older; 57,000 were 12 to 18; 117,000 were under 11; and the ages of the remaining 6,000 were not reported. This surpassed the usual audience in that area for most prime-time evening programs. As a result, the station began to show Laurel and Hardy films at night at prime time.

Artist-writer Larry Byrd produced 11 issues of Pratfall, *a slick 16-page magazine, for the Sons of the Desert's Way Out West tent.*

PRATFALL

THE "WAY OUT WEST" PERIODICAL TRIBUTE TO STAN & OLLIE • VOLUME 1, NUMBER 10 • 5(

The Laurel and Hardy craze has spread far beyond television and theater festivals. In the early 1970s a variety of products bearing the comedians' likenesses were merchandised. Suddenly, the faces of Stan and Ollie were appearing all over: on T-shirts, wrist watches, comic books, jigsaw puzzles, napkins, glasses, calendars, beanies, derbies, hair sprays, spray deodorants, model cars, greeting cards, salt and pepper shakers, records, door mats, towels, pillows, bed sheets, miniature statues, finger puppets, tie clips, cuff links, among other items.

The printing and distribution of "funny money," bearing the faces of Laurel and Hardy, required approval of the U.S. Treasury Department.

A film clip of a Laurel and Hardy movie was used as a television commercial for Hamm's Beer in 1970. In the commercial, using silent screen titles, the comedians walk into a bar and Stan asks for a beer. The bartender asks him what kind he would like. "A beer is a beer," replies Stan in silent print. He then receives the classic exasperated shove from Ollie, and a conventional Hamm's Beersales pitch follows.

Commercials based on Laurel and Hardy film clips were soon made for Standard Oil and Kodak. These advertisements received a great deal of attention. Audiences did not expect to see Laurel and Hardy appearing in television commercials; some thought Laurel and Hardy were actually doing the commercials.

The commercialization of Laurel and Hardy would have certainly increased had not the widows of the two comedians—Lucille Hardy Price and Ida Laurel—and Larry Harmon Pictures Corporation in Hollywood filed suit in 1970 disputing the commercial rights to Laurel and Hardy. In a June, 1975 Manhattan Federal Court statement, Judge Charles Stewart ruled that the widows possessed

Original Laurel and Hardy posters and theatre lobby cards are collectors' treasures. Some are quite valuable.

the rights to merchandise the names and likenesses of the two comedians, rights which Laurel and the widows had assigned exclusively to Larry Harmon in 1961.

The suit revealed that Roach, a California Corporation, a debtor in reorganization under Chapter X of the Bankruptcy Act, originally held copyrights alleged to have been acquired by Roach, a New York corporation, and that these rights included certain employment agreements between Roach-California and Laurel and Hardy. Roach entered into an agreement on May 1, 1969 with Richard Feiner, revised by a later agreement between them, dated January 21, 1971, purporting to convey to Feiner the "world-wide exclusive merchandising rights" to the names and likenesses of Laurel and Hardy. Harmon and the comedians' widows claimed that the defendants were not legally entitled to the rights which they claim, and that their claims are in conflict with the exclusive rights granted to Harmon.

Laurel and Hardy bedspreads, sheets, pillow cases, towels and bathroom accessories were made by Spring Mills.

Larry Harmon, president of Larry Harmon Pictures, producers of *Bozo the Clown*, commented: "All the companies were bidding with Laurel in 1961 for the use of his name, and he picked me. He felt that we could do the best job to perpetuate their name and likeness and style." Harmon received rights for Hardy from his widow. Roach and Feiner had contended that they had gotten the merchandising and commercial rights to Laurel and Hardy prior to 1961.

In August, 1975, a permanent injunction was handed down in Manhattan Federal Court. The defendants were Hal Roach Studios and its licensees, Richard Feiner & Co. Inc., and Overseas Programming Co., Ltd., licensee Richard Feiner personally, and Herbert Gelbspan, officer for Roach Studios, and all persons acting on behalf of the Roach Studios and its licensees. The defendants were "permanently restrained and enjoined from using, selling, licensing, leasing, authorizing the use of . . . the names, likenesses, characters and characterizations of Stan Laurel and Oliver Hardy for advertising, commercial and/or publicity purposes." The defendants were further restrained from using the comedians' likenesses in connection with "publications, recordings, clothing, toys, games, foods, or other products or services, merchandising . . . or in the production of animated cartoons or motion pictures."

Ceramic caricatures of The Fellows, which double as salt and pepper shakers, make a beautiful decorative display.

Jubilant over his victory after a five-year legal battle, Harmon immediately announced that he was going to "Laurel and Hardy-ize" the world. When this book went to press, he was busy working on plans to introduce a variety of Laurel and Hardy products.

"We plan to feature a line of Laurel and Hardy clothing," said Harmon. "This will include blue jeans, sox, sweaters, shirts, T-shirts, tennis shoes and derbies. Many of the items we had on the market during the lawsuit will be continued; others, such as rubber dolls with pop-up hats, hand puppets, string puppets, and school supplies will be improved. Bathroom and bedroom linens and accessories will still be available.

"We will create a line of ceramics, including cookie jars, salt and pepper shakers and decanters. Many kinds of jewelry, including wrist watches, will be made available. Laurel and Hardy greeting cards are in the works. We'll have men's toiletries. We're getting into the food business, too, with frozen Italian foods such as ravioli and lasagna. We'll be franchising Laurel and Hardy Pizza Palaces and Laurel and Hardy Pie Shops across the country. We're also looking into a new line of coffee."

In addition to his other projects, Larry Harmon plans to open more Laurel and Hardy Pizza Palaces and Laurel and Hardy Pie Shops.

Harmon added that one of the biggest projects is the construction of a Laurel and Hardy amusement park. He has also begun work on a fully animated theatrical film, featuring the best of Laurel and Hardy's plots and gags. "This film, which is scheduled to be ready for world-wide distribution in December, 1976, will capture the mood of Laurel and Hardy, including their gestures and voices," he said. Harmon, who is known for the voice he has created for Bozo, the clown, will do the Laurel and Hardy voices himself. Harmon is also negotiating to produce a feature film and a television documentary on the lives of the two men.

Larry Harmon Pictures Corporation plans to produce a full-length animated cartoon feature film for large screen viewing.

The Laurel and Hardy "renaissance" has spread to Europe. On London's Tottenham Court Road in the 1970s, a street salesman was offering Laurel and Hardy T-shirts and cardboard bowler hats and doing brisk business. Laurel and Hardy films are being shown in many foreign countries. A recording made of them singing, "Trail of the Lonesome Pine," from the Laurel and Hardy film,

Laurel and Hardy in a setting at the Movieland Wax Museum in Buena Park, California, a popular tourist attraction.

Way Out West, was No. 2 on England's musical hit parade in 1976.

Laurel and Hardy films are not difficult to obtain. Prints are available from Blackhawk Films, Eastin-Phelan Building, 1235 West Fifth Street, Davenport, Iowa 52808. The prints are licensed for non-theatrical use, home use, and non-theatrical closed circuit television. Blackhawk publishes a bulletin listing the available films and their prices. Prices of the films in 1975 (subject to change) ranged from $17.98 for 400 feet of 8mm of *Flying Elephants* (a 1927 short) to $89.98 for 1,100 feet of 16mm optical sound of *The Music Box* (1932).

Blackhawk has also made available the early films of Stan Laurel. *Half a Man*, produced in 1925, is available for $14.98 (325 feet of standard 8mm). Early Hardy films are also offered, costing from $7.98 to $17.98. Most of the Laurel and Hardy films are usually offered in both 8mm standard and 8mm super for the silents; for the talkies, 16mm was used.

Laurel and Hardy memorabilia is expensive: a one-sheet theater ad poster, 27"x41", dating back to the 1930s, sells for as much as $250; lobby poster inserts, 14"x36", sell for $100 and up; press campaign clip books sell for $25 to $50; and small theater lobby cards are available for $15 and up.

Studio publicity photographs of some of the comedians' films of the 1930s and 1940s are plentiful, but photos of their films dating back to the 1920s and earlier are quite rare. Still more scarce are candid photographs.

Several prints of the film made from their appearance on Ralph Edwards' 1954 *This Is Your Life* television show are in circulation, mostly among members of the Sons of the Desert.

A recording of a telephone interview with Stan Laurel was once considered to be a collector's item, but research by Sons of the Desert in 1973 has revealed that advertising claims that the interview had been made only three weeks (and later eight weeks) before his death were false. The recording was actually made in 1961 by Don Marlowe, who had a television program in Minneapolis. After Laurel's death, he sold the record for $1.00, and later $2.00, via mail order. Hundreds, possibly thousands, were sold.

Jim McNalis of Covina, California sculptured these caricatures of Laurel and Hardy several years ago.

Comedians who impersonate Laurel and Hardy have appeared in night clubs and on television. (Below) A W.C. Fields look-alike is flanked by Stan and Ollie.

A great variety of Laurel and Hardy products are on the market. Shown here are Laurel and Hardy comic books, records, puppets, stamp set, playing cards, stik-ums, Jack-in-the Box, statues, and a scale model car.

Laurel and Hardy were honored with a commemorative star in Hollywood's Walk of Fame. The Walk of Fame, a five-acre sidewalk of charcoal terrazzo embedded at six-foot intervals with coral stars containing the names of entertainment luminaries, extends from Gower Street to Sycamore on Hollywood Boulevard, and from Sunset to Yucca on Vine Street. The Stan Laurel star is located in front of an apartment building at 7021 Hollywood Boulevard, near the London Shop. The Oliver Hardy star can be found at the corner of Sunset and Vine, opposite Wallich's Music City, and in front of the fountain of the Home Saving and Loan Association at 1500 Vine Street.

Life-size figures of Laurel and Hardy can be seen at the Movieland Wax Museum in Buena Park, California, near the famous tourist attractions of Disneyland and Knott's Berry Farm.

A few night club comedy acts based on the Laurel and Hardy characterizations have surfaced in recent years. Some performers bear physical likenesses to Stan and Ollie; many do a noteworthy job of copying their mannerisms. Residents of Pasadena, California were astonished, in 1975, when two night club comedians dressed as Laurel and Hardy walked the city's streets in their derby hats and stand-up collars, imitating the team's well-known gestures.

As the craze continues, Stan and Ollie seem to be alive everywhere. Patrons of a busy Security First National Bank office in Los Angeles can watch Laurel and Hardy films while waiting in line. A few airlines now show Laurel and Hardy animated cartoons that were made by Hanna-Barbera for television several years ago.

The characters and characterizations of Laurel and Hardy are destined to be with us for a long time. The world, after all, can always use a few good laughs.

7.
A Film Review

Forty-Five Minutes from Hollywood, 1926. Most of the scenes take place in a Hollywood hotel. Several Roach comedy stars are featured, including the Our Gang Kids. Hardy plays the house detective; Laurel a starving actor.

Duck Soup, 1927. The plot, adapted from a sketch written by Stan Laurel's father, has Stan fleeing from the police. Hardy plays a very small role in this film, which later was reworked into *Another Fine Mess*, a 1930 talkie.

Slipping Wives, 1927. To make her neglectful husband jealous, a wife asks handyman Stan Laurel to pose as a literary talent and flirt with her. Stan mistakes a guest for the husband and butler Hardy loses his dignity in a paint bucket. Laurel, caught in bed with the wife, is found innocent when the husband discovers the plot.

Love 'Em and Weep, 1927. Jimmy Finlayson, blackmailed by ex-girl friend Mae Busch, enlists the help of business associate Stan Laurel. The effort fails when Mae crashes Finlayson's house party and all the men, including Hardy, a guest, find themselves in hot water with their wives.

Why Girls Love Sailors, 1927. Laurel, disguised as a fancy, jewel-laden female, seeks out Hardy, a sea captain who has run off with Stan's young, exquisite girl friend. Laurel's charms tempt Hardy, but Hardy's wife traps him and Stan and his girl make a getaway.

With Love and Hisses, 1927. As two army recruits Laurel and Hardy are allied against their commanding officer and common enemy, James Finlayson, in a plan to make his life miserable.

Sailors Beware, 1927. When cabdriver Stan Laurel becomes an accidental ship stowaway, he is put to work as a steward. Hardy, the purser, tries to impress the ladies, but Stan is the real hero when he discovers that his former passengers, Anita Garvin and her midget son,are fleecing the passengers out of card money and jewels.

Do Detectives Think? 1927. Detectives Laurel and Hardy guard Judge James

Finlayson from an escaped murderer who sneaks in to replace the butler. Laurel and Hardy are petrified by the murderer's knife-slashing attempts and worry for their own skins. A chance happening leads to the criminal's capture.

Flying Elephants, 1927. Bachelors in the Stone Age have a choice of marriage— or else! Hardy, a sophisticated strong guy, and Laurel, the shy one, both fall for James Finlayson's daughter. In a fight on the cliff, Laurel's victory over Hardy is accomplished by a goat who gives Hardy the push over.

Sugar Daddies, 1927. A nouveau-riche oil man, James Finlayson, discovers through his butler, Hardy, that he was married the previous night. Stan Laurel plays the role of a lawyer and the film evolves around the antics of a blackmailing ring, with much of the film set in an amusement park.

Call of the Cuckoo, 1927. Not only is Max Davidson's long-planned-for home an architectural mess, but it is situated immediately next to an insane asylum. Lunatics Laurel and Hardy and friends come to do tricks on the lawn. The house is ruined as a piano crashes through the walls.

The Second Hundred Years, 1927. Prison inmates Laurel and Hardy escape after borrowing painting gear, clothes and a car, and then realize that they are impersonating the guards of the institution they have just left. After the real officers are arrested for being without clothes, it's back to jail for the convicts.

Hats Off, 1927. Laurel and Hardy are two clumsy handymen whose goal it is to maneuver into a house an unwieldly washing machine that sits on the top of a long flight of steps.

Putting Pants on Philip, 1927. When his nephew arrives on a boat from Scotland, Hardy is horrified to learn that this silly, woman-chasing man in kilts is his relative. All attempts at remedying the situation fail, even that of putting pants on Philip.

The Battle of the Century, 1927. Laurel is a boxer; Hardy his manager. Hardy, doubting Laurel's ability, takes out insurance on his fighter's life, and then sets up an accident. A banana peel is laid out for Laurel, but instead a delivery man trips, and in minutes pies begin flying with everyone becoming involved.

The Finishing Touch, 1928. Stan and Ollie are contractors who build a house which begins to fall apart when a bird settles on its chimney. The customer wants his money back, but the boys object. Rocks are thrown and the house collapses when a brick becomes dislodged.

Leave 'Em Laughing, 1928. In an effort to put his dentist-shy friend Laurel at ease, Hardy sits in the dentist's chair. The busy doctor, without paying heed, extracts Hardy's teeth. Laughing gas sets Laurel and Hardy to uncontrollable giggling. They are still hysterical as they leave and get into their car where they cause a traffic tie-up at which time cop Edgar Kennedy loses his pants.

From Soup to Nuts, 1928. As waiters who have not had much experience, Stan and Babe completely ruin the dinner Anita Garvin had planned for her friends as a showcase for her new-found wealth.

You're Darn Tootin', 1928. Musicians Laurel and Hardy take to the streets after being fired from a city orchestra. Frustration over their failures has Laurel roll Hardy's trombone under a truck. The resulting argument develops into a street free-for-all during which clothes are ripped and pants torn off, including those of the law officers.

Their Purple Moment, 1928. Laurel and Hardy's plans for a night out to go bowling backfire. An accidental meeting with two young ladies, an angry waiter, and a waiting cab-driver keep Laurel from eating, and Hardy from paying the check. When their wives arrive, total bedlam breaks out.

Should Married Men Go Home? 1928. Mr. and Mrs. Hardy are having a peaceful day until Laurel comes along. She gets mad, the boys go golfing, and Sunday ends in havoc because of two charming females and a hotheaded Edgar Kennedy.

Early to Bed, 1928. When Hardy becomes an heir and gives his friend Stan a job as butler, he immediately uses his new status in life to torment Laurel. When Stan discovers that by damaging a piece of Hardy's new furniture he can get revenge, he sets his plan into motion.

Two Tars, 1928. Sailors Laurel and Hardy on a Sunday leave are sporting two dates and raring to go when they run into a traffic jam. Hardy lets loose! The motorists do the same. They decide to chase the two instigators and, as they enter an empty tunnel, they are met by a train coming towards them.

Habeas Corpus, 1928. Stan and Babe have jobs working for a very friendly, but demented, scientist, Richard Carle. For his experiments he needs corpses and The Fellows are called upon to supply them.

We Faw Down, 1928. While Laurel and Hardy are out playing poker, their wives think the boys were burned in a theater fire. Their grief turns to anger when they discover that their husbands, after falling in the mud, are being cared for in the apartment of two lovely dames.

Liberty, 1929. Laurel and Hardy, aided in a prison break by friends, exchange their convict garb for street clothes in the getaway car. They soon realize that their pants have been switched. Efforts to change lead them into odd situations, and in the end they find themselves high up on a skyscraper—but all ends well.

Wrong Again, 1929. Working in a stable, Laurel and Hardy think that "Blue Boy" is a horse. When a reward is offered for the painting's return, they bring the animal to the owner of Blue Boy who calls from upstairs to put it on the piano. The boys struggle to get the horse on the piano.

That's My Wife, 1929. Hardy's claim to his uncle's fortune can only be kept alive so long as he is married. Since his wife has already abandoned him, Babe has Stan impersonate her, as the "couple" takes the uncle to a nightclub. The secret finally slips out, and Hardy's hopes of becoming wealthy fade away.

Big Business, 1929. Selling Christmas trees in July in California is not a successful venture for salesmen Laurel and Hardy. With the help of James Finlayson, they set out to prove that it can be done. Sales not only fail to materialize, but a lot of rough stuff heaps ruin upon Finlayson's home and the boys' business.

Double Whoopee, 1929. Doormen Laurel and Hardy's arrival at a New York hotel is mistaken for that of royalty. The plush treatment that is accorded them is quickly withdrawn upon the arrival of the prince, and they are ordered to take up their jobs.

Berth Marks, 1929. As itinerant musicians traveling on trains, Laurel and Hardy play in one hick town after another. When their station is unexpectedly called, they run from the train, still undressed. As the train departs, they realize that their instruments are still on board.

Men O'War, 1929. Laurel and Hardy, sailors on leave, try to enjoy themselves with two girls and only fifteen cents between them. A slot machine gives Laurel the money they need and, with it, The Fellows try their seamanship on a boat. Collisions and arguments make the boys very unpopular.

A Perfect Day, 1929. Edgar Kennedy, who would rather stay home with a sore foot, is persuaded by Laurel and Hardy and their wives to go on a picnic. Their car gets stuck in a mudhole and, from then on, it's downhill.

They Go Boom, 1929. Laurel wants to help Ollie recover from a head cold and tries everything—including hopping into bed with him. Nothing helps, and the room is soon a shambles.

Bacon Grabbers, 1929. Having been served a summons, Laurel and Hardy hunt up Edgar Kennedy. They try to avoid his ferocious dog as they seek to have the unpaid-for radio returned to him, but Kennedy continues to elude them.

Angora Love, 1929. Although no pets are allowed in The Fellows' rented room, they bring in a goat they've found because rumor has it that the goat's been stolen, and they are afraid they will be blamed. Their attempts to fool the landlord don't work.

Unaccustomed As We Are, 1929. Hardy's wife leaves, rather than cook for Laurel. The next door neighbor, a jealous policeman's wife, offers them a meal. Her dress gets burned, and off it comes. When the cop and Mrs. Hardy arrive, it's into the trunk for her.

Hollywood Review of 1929, 1929. Primarily musical, this film has Hardy in the role of a magician, only to have a very clumsy Laurel ruin everything he attempts.

Hoosegow, 1929. Stan and Babe, cowardly convicts, dig ditches and work with a road gang. James Finlayson, a prison inspector, does not find out that they have ruined his car radiator which they filled with rice. The boiling water sets off an explosion.

Night Owls, 1930. Cop Edgar Kennedy makes a pact with hobos Laurel and Hardy. Kennedy has been unable to catch any thieves, but if the two hobos will burglarize his chief's home, Kennedy can be a hero and they will be provided with safe exit. Nothing goes right; even Kennedy gets arrested.

Blotto, 1930. During prohibition, Laurel and Hardy, not knowing that Mrs. Hardy has filled it with her own drinking blend, take their special bottle to a club. They become drunk and are sublimely happy, until Mrs. Hardy arrives with a shotgun and destroys their getaway car.

Rogue Song, 1930. Based on an operetta, the film stars Lawrence Tibbett as a Russian bandit-ruler, who loves a princess and kills her brother. Laurel and

Hardy add the comedy touches.

Be Big, 1930. While their wives are away, Laurel and Hardy plan to attend an Atlantic City convention. Since riding habits are the required dress for this particular visit to the seashore, they spend all their time trying to don pants and boots and never do make it outdoors.

Brats, 1930. Laurel and Hardy's wives have left them babysitting for their two sons, each a tiny replica of his father. The comedians play both fathers and babies.

Below Zero, 1930. Street musicians Laurel and Hardy are not greeted with enthusiasm when they play "Good Old Summertime" in a snowstorm. But luck is with them when they find a lost wallet. To help them enjoy a bountiful meal, the local cop is invited. But the wallet belongs to the cop, and the boys go into hiding.

The Laurel & Hardy Murder Case, 1930. When Hardy discovers that Laurel is an heir, the two go to a spooky, ancient house to collect the valuables. Hardy panics when he thinks that he sees ghosts and killers. He discovers that it is only a dream.

Hog Wild, 1930. Hardy's wife wants him to install a radio aerial on the roof, but Babe's clumsiness makes her nervous. To prove who's boss, he ignores her and calls on Laurel for help.

Another Fine Mess, 1930. Finlayson, a rich wild game hunter, expects his servants to rent his house while he's away. But the servants do not remain in the house, and Laurel and Hardy, who are hiding from the authorities, settle in. When a couple, interested in renting the house, arrives, Hardy pretends to be the owner, Laurel the maid. Finlayson's unexpected return uncovers the deception.

Chickens Come Home, 1931. Businessman Hardy has just been married, and he gets Laurel to help when an old girl friend tries to blackmail him. Not to be deterred, she comes to his house and Mrs. Hardy can't be convinced.

Laughing Gravy, 1931. Stan and Babe hide a dog in their apartment. When the landlord protests that it is against the rules, they throw the pet into the snow, and then try to retrieve him. A smallpox quarantine, the landlord's suicide, and the couple's zany antics give their apartment a totally madhouse appearance.

Our Wife, 1931. Although rich James Finlayson wants to get rid of his fat, dumb daughter, Oliver Hardy is still not good enough for her. Hardy gets Laurel to help him elope. But, when the ceremony is over, it's Laurel who is the bridegroom.

Come Clean, 1931. The Laurels visit the Hardys and the boys go to the store for ice cream. On the way, they save Mae Busch from drowning. Because she holds them responsible for saving her life, they hide her in the bathroom. The wives find out. Hardy blames Laurel, but, when Mae turns out to be an escaped maniac, Laurel gets the reward.

Pardon Us, 1931. Bootleggers Laurel and Hardy go to jail where Laurel's loose tooth creates a raspberry sound that makes the most feared inmate think that Laurel's a brave man. The Fellows escape from prison, but soon get caught; Laurel's raspberry stops a riot, and he is pardoned as a reward.

Upon his release, Laurel returns to his old life-style of bootlegging.

One Good Turn, 1931. This movie takes place during the depression and Laurel and Hardy not only travel in their car, but live in it. In a small town, they overhear some rehearsal dialogue which they mistake for a threat by James Finlayson to dispossess a widow who has befriended them. They sell their car, present her with the money, only to discover that they need it more than she does.

Beau Hunks, 1931. Legionnaires Laurel and Hardy enlist in the Foreign Legion in hopes of forgetting Hardy's unfortunate love affair. When the ex-flame turns out to have been everyone's sweetheart, they decide to resign. The commanding officer is enraged, but, when they mine the field with thumb tacks before the enemy attacks, they are hailed as heroes.

Helpmates, 1931. Because Hardy does not want his wife to know what he has been doing while she has been away, he and Laurel remove the traces of some wild fun. Laurel's efforts ruin Hardy's clothes, make the returning wife mad, and reduce the house to a smoking shambles.

Any Old Port, 1931. While sailors Laurel and Hardy are on leave, Laurel tries to earn money as a boxer so that the pretty girl who makes their beds won't have to marry the monstrous hotel owner. His boxing opponent turns out to be the bridegroom. Laurel comes through with a win, but the girl runs off with her boyfriend.

The Music Box, 1932. The Fellows transport a cart to a hilltop. The piano it carries is a birthday surprise. The homeowner hates pianos, and destroys it before he discovers that it is a gift for his wife. In the process, the boys wreck his home. The man decides that he'll pay for the piano anyway, but, as he prepares to do so, his pen backfires.

The Chimp, 1932. When the circus closes down, Laurel receives the flea circus as his salary, and the trained chimp goes to Hardy. By coincidence, the landlord's wife has the same name as the chimp's, and Hardy is confronted by the irate husband who thinks Hardy is calling his wife to go to bed. As the husband gets his gun, the human Ethel arrives, and the chimp ends up with the weapon.

County Hospital, 1932. Hardy's accident has put him in the hospital, and a visit from Laurel does not improve his physical condition. Stan causes mayhem with the doctor, Billy Gilbert, who discharges Hardy even though he is not fit to leave. Stan then accidentally sits on a hypodermic needle, which makes him sleepy. Nevertheless, he drives Hardy home and a wild ride through heavy traffic ensues.

Scram, 1932. Vagrants Laurel and Hardy are ordered by the local judge to leave town. As they are standing in the rain, a well-meaning drunk invites them home. Accidentally, they are taken to the judge's house, where the boys' innocent but suspicious encounter with the wife causes an uproar.

Pack Up Your Troubles, 1932. Before their best friend is killed in World War I, The Fellows promise him they'll care for his little girl and return her to her rich grandparents. The name is Smith, and finding the couple is difficult, especially since the orphanage officials are trying to take the child away.

Their First Mistake, 1932. Laurel decides the Hardys won't have any more fights if they adopt a baby. But when the two men bring back the infant, they find Mrs. Hardy has left for good, and they're stuck with feeding and putting the infant to sleep.

Towed in a Hole, 1933. When Laurel and Hardy realize that the Hollywood residents won't buy the fish they peddle in the streets, they decide to buy a boat—their idea being that they can make better business deals if they catch their own fish. They set out on their boat and a breeze whisks the boat to destruction.

Twice Two, 1933. The Hardys and the Laurels are having an anniversary dinner with the boys playing double roles: Laurel as Hardy's wife, and Hardy as Laurel's. A whole mess of marital quarreling ensues.

Me and My Pal, 1933. Hardy decides to insure his recent success as a moneyed executive by marrying the boss' daughter, but best man Laurel brings him a jigsaw puzzle. They start to play with it and, become so absorbed, they never make the church. The wedding is cancelled, and the almost completed puzzle is destroyed.

Fra Diavola (The Devil's Brother), 1933. This is Auber's operetta in burlesque. Bandit Fra Diavola, held up by vagrants Laurel and Hardy, decides to use them in his fraudulent scheme. Stan reveals the identity of the bandit, but the three are ordered to be shot. Laurel saves the day with a red handkerchief that brings out a bull, and everyone escapes.

The Midnight Patrol, 1933. As patrol cops, Stan and Ollie work hard, but are not too bright. They arrest a prowler who turns out to be the police chief trying to get into his own house.

Busy Bodies, 1933. Laurel and Hardy enjoy their jobs as employees in a woodworking shop. Their usual bumbling ways get them fired by the time the film ends.

Dirty Work, 1933. The boys play chimney sweeps at the home of a crazy scientist, Lucien Littlefield, who has just made an egg out of a duck. With Laurel's help, Hardy, playing with the formula, turns into a chimpanzee.

Sons of the Desert, 1934. Laurel and Hardy tell their wives that they're going on a sea trip, but, in fact, they are off to a convention. When their wives learn that a ship has been wrecked, they go into mourning. Then, they see a newsreel of their husbands—alive and having fun at the convention. When the boys return home, they pretend to have escaped from the bottom of the ocean.

The Private Life of Oliver the Eighth, 1934. Barbers Laurel and Hardy want to get rich. Hardy offers himself as a husband candidate to a well-to-do widow. Unfortunately, she is obsessed with murdering men who have the name "Oliver." A knife at his throat awakens Hardy, but it's all only a dream.

Hollywood Party, 1934. Laurel and Hardy are featured players in this musical comedy revue. In one of their routines, Hardy, with the help of Laurel's whispered instructions, shows glamorous Lupe Velez how to break an egg.

Going Bye Bye, 1934. When killer Walter Long escapes, The Fellows, the trial's star witnesses, leave town. They advertise for someone to share expenses with them. The ad is responded to by the killer's sweetheart. The unsuspecting boys don't know that the killer is hiding in her trunk. They help get him out, and Long gets his revenge before the police arrive.

Them Thar Hills, 1934. Laurel and Hardy, camping in the mountains for Hardy's health, find very "potent" well water, unaware that it is dumped bootlegger's liquor. Charlie Hall, his car out of gas, leaves wife Mae Busch with the boys, who invite her to share the liquid refreshment. Hall returns to find his wife drunk and a battle follows.

Babes in Toyland, 1934. Stan and Ollie are the toymaker's helpers. When the villain, Barnaby, tries to take over Toyland, the huge wooden soldiers Laurel and Hardy have accidentally created are put in command. Barnaby is defeated and expelled from Toyland.

The Live Ghost, 1934. Fish cannery workers Laurel and Hardy are recruited by the captain of a suspected ghost ship to kidnap a crew; they are hauled in with the others. Believing they have killed their cabin mate, The Fellows throw him into the sea only to have him return. Everyone yells the captain's hated word, "ghost," and punishment is meted out.

Tit for Tat, 1934. Playing electrical appliance store owners, Laurel and Hardy try to exchange free services with delicatessen store neighbor Charlie Hall, only to learn that they had once done battle with him on a camping trip. Hardy is freakishly catapulted into Mrs. Hall's bedroom. Hall is enraged and the stores' merchandise is converted into a mess.

The Fixer Uppers, 1935. Laurel and Hardy play greeting card salesmen who let a customer persuade Hardy to make her artist-husband jealous. The scheme backfires when the husband demands satisfaction in a duel. Stan and Ollie get drunk and a cabdriver mistakenly delivers them to the customer's house. The husband finds them and attempts to murder them.

Thicker Than Water, 1935. Laurel persuades Hardy to be the master in his home. Hardy withdraws all the money from his bank account, and buys a clock which is smashed by a truck. Mrs. Hardy's anger puts Oliver in the hospital, and Stan reluctantly donates blood.

Bonnie Scotland, 1935. When a young, Scottish friend enlists in the army, so do Laurel and Hardy. The young friend's girl follows them to India, but the romance is disturbed by rioting natives.

The Bohemian Girl, 1936. Laurel and Hardy play Bohemian gypsies in this film about a nobleman's daughter kidnapped and brought up by gypsies. Unaware of her heritage, she is accused of stealing from her father. A reunion takes place when her true identity is disclosed.

Our Relations, 1936. As spendthrift sailors, going on leave, Laurel and Hardy ask the captain to hold their money while they deliver a diamond ring. The port is the home of their long lost twin brothers, now married. The boys find two girls, run into the relatives, lose the ring, and get involved with gangsters. In the end, the brothers reunite.

Way Out West, 1937. When Stan and Ollie come to deliver a deed to a gold mine to their dead partner's daughter, saloon-keeper James Finlayson passes off his partner as the heiress. The real heiress is the kitchenmaid. While attempting to set things right, the boys are chased away, but things work out well in the end.

Pick a Star, 1937. Laurel and Hardy portray themselves in a film in which a pretty young girl, Rosina Lawrence, achieves stardom. Jack Haley, her publicity man, helps it all come true.

Swiss Miss, 1938. Mousetrap salesmen, played by Laurel and Hardy, arrive in Switzerland to sell their wares in the land of Swiss cheese. A hotel cook, furious with their poor demonstrations, forces them to work in the kitchen. Their enforced stay has a plus: they patch up a romance between two singers at a town festival.

Blockheads, 1938. Twenty years after World War I, Laurel, unaware of peace, is found in the trench Hardy left him to guard. When Hardy brings Stan home, his wife leaves. Laurel wrecks everything he touches and involves himself and Ollie with a neighboring blonde. When Mrs. Hardy and the girl's husband return, out come the shotguns.

The Flying Deuces, 1939. Jilted by his sweetheart, Hardy plots suicide. A Foreign Legion soldier induces Laurel and Hardy to enlist. The soldier's wife is discovered to be Hardy's ex-girl. As soldiers, Laurel and Hardy are inept, and orders to shoot them are issued. They escape and crash in a plane. Laurel lives but Hardy dies, returning to this world as a horse.

A Chump at Oxford, 1940. When street cleaners Laurel and Hardy prevent a bank robbery, they are sent to Oxford University to study, as a reward. During a hazing, a blow to the head causes Laurel to behave like a famous British genius. He makes Hardy his slave, but a window slams on Laurel's head, returning him to his normal mental state.

Saps at Sea, 1940. As employees of a horn factory, The Fellows seek a respite from the noise. Following Dr. Finlayson's suggestion, who recommends a rest at sea, the boys board a boat. An escaped killer is captured when Laurel blows a horn, but, upon hearing the noise, Hardy goes wild. Laurel is a hero until he reveals the secret of his bravery. After combat with the police, Hardy is jailed.

Great Guns, 1941. Laurel and Hardy, guards of a rich man's son, think it unwise for him to be in the army by himself, so, when he gets drafted, they enter the service with him. The playboy proves fully capable of taking care of himself, but Laurel and Hardy get into trouble with the sergeant.

A-Haunting We Will Go, 1942. Stan and Ollie are tricked into being coffin escorts for a leader of a gang who is trying to elude the police. While escorting the coffin, a switch takes place, leaving the boys with the one used in a magic act. The crooks chase them, but the boys make the capture.

Air Raid Wardens, 1943. As air raid wardens during the war, Laurel and Hardy learn of the Nazis' plans to damage a magnesium factory. The plot revolves around their prevention efforts and their ultimate success.

Jitterbugs, 1943. Stan and Ollie decide to ensure the success of a girl night club singer challenging some shady characters who are doing their best to wreck her career.

The Dancing Masters, 1943. Two dancing school operators, played by Laurel and Hardy, befriend an inventor. To make money, Hardy insures Laurel with crooked brokers. The Fellows break up the gang and help their young inventor friend.

The Big Noise, 1944. Janitors Laurel and Hardy work for a detective agency. Pretending to be sharp investigators, they land jobs guarding the inventor of a super bomb. After eluding enemy agents, they sink a Japanese submarine with the bomb.

Nothing But Trouble, 1944. When spies try to kill a young boy who is really a deposed monarch, chef Laurel and butler Hardy, who work in high society, emerge as heroes.

The Bullfighters, 1945. While private detectives Laurel and Hardy are looking for a lady crook in Mexico, Laurel is asked to substitute for a matador who has disappeared and whom he resembles. While Laurel faces the bull, the missing matador returns and total confusion results.

Atoll K*, 1951. Stan and Babe inherit a yacht and an island. A storm wrecks the ship but an atoll appears. When uranium is found, the entire world battles for ownership of the atoll. Eventually, the boys find their island, but high taxes ruin their hopes for a comfortable life.

*Released also as *Robinson Crusoeland* in 1952 and as *Utopia* in 1954.

(Top) In their 1928 film, The Finishing Touch, *Laurel and Hardy played carpenters. (Bottom) One of the 14 films the comedy team made for Hal Roach Studios in 1927 was* The Second Hundred Years.

Laurel and Hardy could provoke audience laughter even with their backs to the camera, as these scenes (top from Habeas Corpus; bottom from Berth Marks) so graphically reveal.

(Above) Ollie encounters problems in Habeas Corpus as a cemetery wall he scales suddenly collapses beneath him. (Left) Hardy finds himself in another fine mess from wet paint in this scene from Habeas Corpus, a two-reeler released in 1928.

Hardy, with the help of Laurel, tries to erect a radio aerial on the roof of his home in Hog Wild, a 1930 two-reeler.

(Above) Hardy's attempt to install an aerial in Hog Wild ends in his falling down a chimney amid a shower of bricks and soot. (Below) Refusing to abandon his efforts, Hardy and his pal, Laurel, find themselves in still deeper trouble.

Puncturing of dignity, the secret of slapstick comedy, keynoted the team's films, as in this incident in That's My Wife.

This was the wild street scene in The Battle of the Century. *More than 2,000 pies were thrown in the melee.*

Do-it-yourself tooth extraction can be a scary and painful experience, as Laurel discovers in Leave 'Em Laughing.

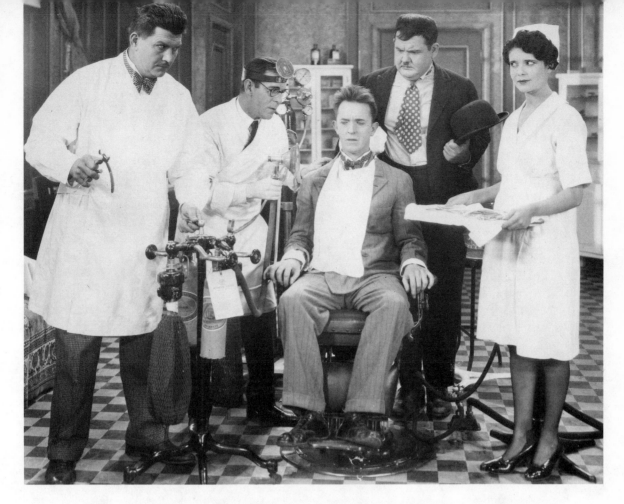

(Above) Laurel is quite concerned about facing extraction of his teeth and receiving an anesthetic in Leave 'Em Laughing. (Below) In another scene from Leave 'Em Laughing, *Laurel and Hardy* fail to take a traffic cop seriously, after accidentally receiving laughing gas from a dentist.

Laurel and Hardy, playing sailors on leave in Two Tars, rent a car and run into a
traffic jam that results in the destruction of several cars.

Men O' War, made in 1929, contains a hilarious conversation between Hardy and a girl about lost gloves and panties.

In Big Business, *Laurel and Hardy play Christmas tree salesmen who call at the home of Jimmy Finlayson. Trouble soon erupts.*

Double Whoopee, *made in 1929, marked the first screen appearance of Jean Harlow, who loses part of her dress in a taxi door.*

Lupe Velez got her start as an actress by appearing in Laurel and Hardy films. This scene was from Hollywood Party.

Laurel breaks into tears in an early film. Crying soon became his trademark.

Planning to meet at a train depot, Stan and Ollie narrowly miss each other repeatedly in *Berth Marks. Disaster results.*

In Brats, *The Fellows portray adults who act as baby sitters while their wives are away. They also play the children.*

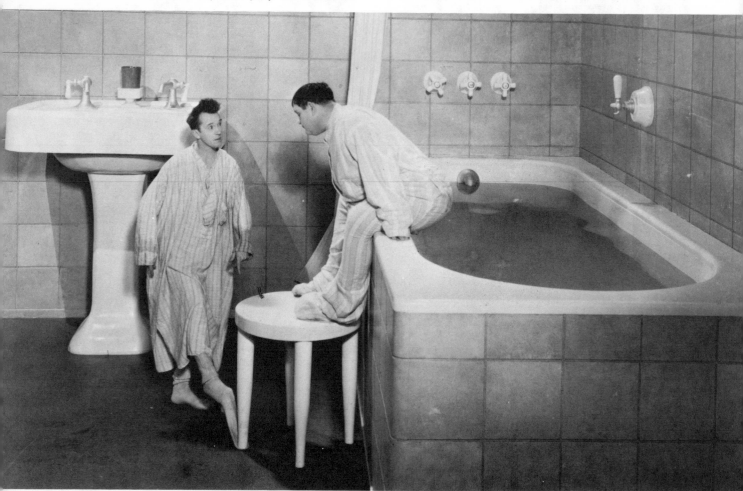

(Above) In The Second Hundred Years, *Laurel and Hardy try to dig their way out of prison, but end up in the warden's office. (Left) Stan inevitably got Ollie into some kind of trouble. A* Perfect Day *was no exception.*

After escaping from prison in Pardon Us, *Stan and Ollie impersonate plantation workers. They run into the warden, who has had car trouble.*

(Above) Fra Diavolo (The Devil's Brother) *was a humorous burlesque of a famous operetta. Made in 1933, it was one of the team's best pictures. (Below) In this scene from* The Laurel and Hardy Murder Case, *Laurel and Hardy go to an old house to claim a fortune which Stan has inherited.*

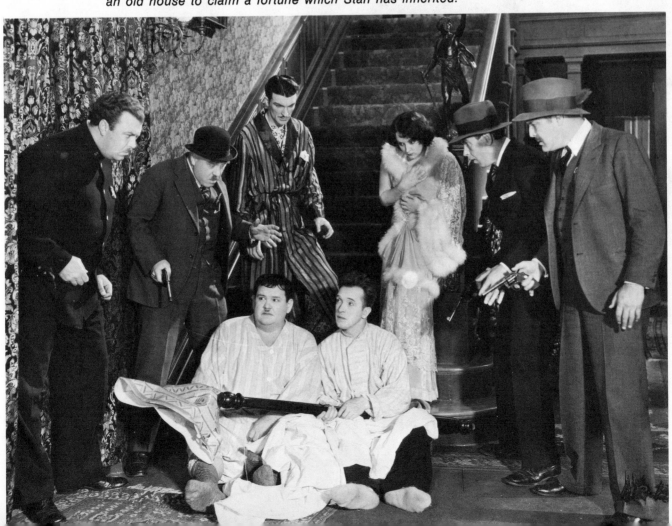

Laurel and Hardy played struggling musicians in You're Darn Tootin'. Losing their jobs, they become street musicians.

Moving a heavy piano over a narrow swaying suspension bridge is tough
enough without meeting a gorilla, as they do in Swiss Miss.

(Above) This humorous scene, with Tom Kennedy (at left), was deleted from Liberty, a 1929 film. (Below) Our Wife, a 1931 film, in which Hardy stages an elopement with a millionaire's daughter, contains many funny scenes.

(Top) In Beau Hunks, *a four-reeler made in 1931, the comedians join the* Foreign Legion so that Hardy can forget a tragic love affair. *(Bottom) Mae* Busch gives Laurel a trying moment as he attempts to help Hardy in Chickens Come Home, *released in 1931.*

(Left) Stan and Ollie play greeting card salesmen in The Fixer Uppers. *They meet Mae Busch, who is married to an artist who neglects her. (Below)* Tit for Tat *produces many laughs for Laurel and Hardy fans. The Fellows portray owners of a new electrical appliance store.*

In Bonnie Scotland, *Laurel and Hardy journey from America to Scotland to collect an inheritance. There, they join an Army regiment.*

(Above) Pick a Star, *made in 1937, included Mischa Auer (fourth from left),* Jack Haley *(center), and* Patsy Kelley *(right).*

(Below) *In* Chump at Oxford, *Laurel and Hardy foil a bank robbery and receive a reward—an education at England's Oxford University.*

(Right) Stan and Ollie again join the Foreign Legion for a series of escapades in The Flying Deuces, *released in 1939. (Below) Laurel and Hardy are drafted into the service in* Great Guns, *made by Twentieth Century-Fox in 1941. The beautiful onlooker is Sheila Ryan.*

Laurel and Hardy portrayed wardens who foil a Nazi plot in Air Raid Wardens, *a 1943 MGM film.*

Reviewers gave Air Raid Wardens little praise and cited it as being repetitious and having childish appeal only.

The Big Noise, a 1944 Twentieth Century-Fox film, found Laurel and Hardy playing janitors for a private detective agency.

Laurel was 54 years old and Hardy was 52 when they made Nothing But Trouble for MGM in 1944.